THREE PLAYS

BY BETH HENLEY

CONTROL FREAKS
L-PLAY
SISTERS OF THE WINTER MADRIGAL

★

★

DRAMATISTS
PLAY SERVICE
INC.

TABLE OF CONTENTS

CONTROL FREAKS

CONTROL FREAKS was given its world premiere by Center Theater in Chicago, Illinois, in 1992. It was directed by the author; the set design was by Rob Hamilton; the lighting design was by Chris Phillips; the costume design was by Lynn Sandberg; the sound design/original music was by Joe Cerqua. The cast was as follows:

SISTER (SPAGHETTI/PINKIE) WILLARD .... Robin Witt
BETTY WILLARD .... Marlene DuBois
CARL WILLARD .... Marc Vann
PAUL CASPER .... Champ Clark

CONTROL FREAKS was produced by the Met Theatre in Los Angeles, California, in 1993. It was directed by the author and produced by David Beard and Holly Hunter; the set design was by Neal Patel; the lighting design was by Rand Ryan; the costume design was by Ruth Myers and Luke Reiche; the sound design/original music was by Joe Cerqua. The cast was as follows:

SISTER (SPAGHETTI/PINKIE) WILLARD .... Holly Hunter
BETTY WILLARD .... Carol Kane
CARL WILLARD .... Bill Pullman
PAUL CASPER .... Wayne Pere

CHARACTERS

SISTER (SPAGHETTI/PINKIE) WILLARD — 30s, has just returned from jury duty

BETTY WILLARD — 40s, Sister's sister-in-law, Carl's wife

CARL WILLARD — 40s, Sister's brother, Betty's husband

PAUL CASPER — 20s–30s, the guest

PLACE

The play takes place in the Willard home in Los Angeles.

The set is divided into three areas: The kitchen; the yard; Sister's upstairs bedroom.

A strange carrot garden in the yard.

In Sister's room there is a bed-chair (a chair that is designed to look like a bed) and several cheap wigs on wig stands. There is a large window in her room that overlooks the yard.

The set should be a frightening combination of dream/real, fake/real and real. Everything should be kept extremely spare. Basically, if it is not used in the play, don't put it on the set.

TIME

Now.

AUTHOR'S NOTE to actress playing Sister: Sister has no knowledge of Spaghetti or Pinkie. Pinkie knows there is Spaghetti. Spaghetti knows there is Pinkie and Sister.

CONTROL FREAKS

Carl and Sister's house. Betty, forties, sits at the kitchen table dressed in a sunny, crisp housedress with a full skirt. The table is set for tea for two with china from a toy tea set. Betty stares morosely at the tiny tea setting. It is late afternoon.

Sister sits in her bedroom. Her white legs are bare. There is a tattoo on her arm of a face without eyes surrounded by a cracked heart.

SISTER. This is my window. I've been gone for some time. I was on jury duty. We were sequestered. We all stayed together at a convenient motel. We all wore badges. When our case was over, we had to return the badges. We couldn't just keep them like they were a souvenir. The government owns them. They're public property. Still we were able to get quite a bit of wear out of our badges. It was a lengthy deliberation. But, finally, today we sentenced the man in handcuffs. They had him in handcuffs. He had to sit there in front of everyone wearing handcuffs. The rest of us could raise our arms, but he couldn't. He got a lot of time. We decided to throw the book at him. He had come to no good. That's where chance had taken him and it was too late to change his habits. There was no way to break his patterns. He was a bad egg. A rotten apple in a barrel. You might as well spit at him as look at him. I'm sorry to say this man was less than dirt and we had to put him away for good. It was an easy decision. Like choosing chocolate over vanilla. *(Betty suddenly smiles eagerly. Her eyes become bright and cheerful. She rings a little dinner bell.)*
BETTY. Teatime! It's teatime! Your tea is served!
SISTER. *(Spaghetti/Pinkie.)* [SP] Fucking teatime./ [P] Be nice./ [SP] Choke shit. *(Sister comes down the stairs and enters the kitchen.)*
BETTY. Hello! Tea's ready!

SISTER. Oh goody! How pretty! Isn't this adorable! Isn't this cute!

BETTY. You deserve it. You've been working hard.

SISTER. I enjoy hard work. It's good for you. Keeps you honest.

BETTY. Yes, yes. Always have your nose to the grindstone.

SISTER. And what do you do?

BETTY. Me?

SISTER. Uh-huh. For a living?

BETTY. Oh, for money?

SISTER. Yeah.

BETTY. I teach cold reading classes.

SISTER. Cold reading classes?

BETTY. Yes. It's for actors. I train actors. That's how I met Carl.

SISTER. Carl's not an actor.

BETTY. He's got a lot of very good potential. He did a scene from *Major Dad* that absolutely oozed with potential. Do you like lemon or cream?

SISTER. It's tea, right?

BETTY. Yes, tea.

SISTER. I don't put cream in tea. When I think of cream, I think cream is for coffee.

BETTY. Well, how about sugar?

SISTER. Sugar is good. That can go in tea.

BETTY. Lemon and sugar then?

SISTER. Good. Fine. Whatever you say. It's your tea; you made it.

BETTY. All right. Fine. This is very nice.

SISTER. Yes, having tea and all. Having a spot of tea. Carl tell you anything? He say anything about me?

BETTY. He told me he had a sister.

SISTER. Yes. We're a close-knit family. Carl gets married and goes off sometimes. He'll marry someone for awhile, then he comes back to me and Mother.

BETTY. I was sorry to hear about Mother's accident.

SISTER. It was a cruel blow.

BETTY. Carl says.

SISTER. I was just grateful he was here when it happened.

BETTY. It's good to have a man around the house.

SISTER. Yeah. It's good to have a man around the house.

BETTY. Would you like a ginger snap?

SISTER. Do we have any ice cream?

BETTY. Oh, yes.

SISTER. What kind?

BETTY. Chocolate.

SISTER. Good. That's good. We like chocolate ice cream. It's our favorite.

BETTY. I'm afraid —

SISTER. What?

BETTY. There's only enough left for Carl's shake. When he comes home he likes his shake.

SISTER. I know about his shake. I know he likes his shake.

BETTY. Well. I have the ginger snaps.

SISTER. These things'll break your teeth. They make houses out of this stuff.

BETTY. I'm sorry about the ice cream.

SISTER. It's not good to be low on ice cream.

BETTY. I'll go to the store.

SISTER. What for?

BETTY. Ice cream.

SISTER. Well, that's not a bad idea. It's not good to be low on ice cream.

BETTY. Is there anything else I should get?

SISTER. The last thing I need is a carton of cigarettes. Camel unfiltered. I don't want them in this house. I don't wanna get cancer of the throat. That is something I could live without.

BETTY. Don't worry, this is a smoke-free house. No smoking is allowed. See, I put up this sampler.

SISTER. Let me see that. You put this up?

BETTY. Yes.

SISTER. You hung it on a nail?

BETTY. Yes.

SISTER. So you put that nail in the wall?

BETTY. To hang the picture.

SISTER. But you don't live here; you don't live here.

BETTY. I'm staying here.

SISTER. Temporarily. Till you get another place. You were evicted, right? You got kicked out on Christmas Day. Carl related it all to me. He picked up you and your Christmas tree and brought

11

you over here. Temporarily.

BETTY. We're married now.

SISTER. What?

BETTY. Carl and me got married in Las Vegas at the Elvis Presley Chapel. It was a spur-of-the-moment decision. Our next plan is to go off on a honeymoon to Maui and drink out of cut-up pieces of fruit.

SISTER. Well, isn't this a nice surprise?

BETTY. Yes, it is.

SISTER. And so sudden. Isn't it sudden? A sudden thing.

BETTY. Carl's the one. He swept me off my feet. "Why put off till tomorrow what you can do today?" he said to me.

SISTER. Yes, that's a good point, a point well taken. But you've caught me off guard. I'm embarrassed. I should have a wedding present for you. I should have brought you a gift.

BETTY. Oh, not to worry. We're going to throw a big reception after the honeymoon, so we'll have a chance to celebrate with all of those we love and treasure.

SISTER. Am I invited to the reception?

BETTY. Well, I'm not sure. It hasn't been discussed. We haven't decided on the invites.

SISTER. Where're my cats? Have you seen my cats?

BETTY. Those two fat cats?

SISTER. Garfield and Plums.

BETTY. Why, those are the fattest cats I've ever seen. They're so fat I entered their picture in a contest.

SISTER. What contest?

BETTY. The fat cat photo contest. I thought they were sure to win first prize, but they lost.

CARL. *(Offstage.)* Hey, Honey! Baby! Sugar Snaps!

BETTY. Oh, there's Carl! *(Carl, forties, enters. He wears a cheap suit and carries a plastic briefcase. He wears black glasses and has on a curly hairpiece.)*

CARL. *(Spotting Sister.)* Oh my goodness! Look who's back!

SISTER. Look who's married!

CARL. Pop goes the weasel!

BETTY. I'll fix your shake.

CARL. You know it, Babe. *(To Sister, about Betty.)* Isn't she a winner? Am I a lucky gun?

SISTER. Bang, bang, bang!

CARL. Shoot 'em up! Rawhide! Hey, how was the trial?

SISTER. Oh, he was a bad man. A rotten apple in a barrel. You wouldn't have liked him, Carl. Not one bit. We socked him away for life. I wanted to watch him fry. But they only let you give him life.

CARL. Well, I'm proud of you, Sister. You've done a public service. Good for you, Little Rascal. *(To Betty.)* Did I tell you I had a sister, or what?

BETTY. Oh yes, and now that Sister's back we can cinch the deal.

CARL. Cinch the deal! All right!

SISTER. What deal?

CARL. Furniture World?

SISTER. Huh?

CARL. I'm opening up a giant furniture market. Don't worry, Little Scampy, you're in. I'm gonna let you work the floor. Here, check out these brochures, these order forms. What do you think? I'm a big fan of this modular bedroom set. It's virtually carefree. It's all been treated with Stain Safe. It's completely soil repellent.

SISTER. But, Carl, I wanted to open up a Frosty Shop. Remember all the frozen delights we invented? We don't know anything about furniture.

CARL. What're you talking? I've been around furniture all my life. What do you think? You need a degree to plop your behind on some foam rubber?!

SISTER. If Mother was here, she'd say this is just another one of your harebrained schemes.

CARL. Mother's not here.

SISTER. No. *(Betty turns on the shake machine. It makes a loud, shrieking, monstrous sound that only Sister is aware of. Betty pours the shake into a glass and hands it to Carl.)*

BETTY. Here's your shake, honey. *(Carl picks up his shake, takes a small sip, then sets it down.)* Don't you like it? *(Carl shrugs non-committally.)*

SISTER. Maybe she didn't make it right. I know how you —

CARL. She made it right. She makes the best shakes I've ever had. *(Carl now makes a big deal out of slurping up his delicious shake as he continues to pout. Sister picks up the brochures and starts looking through them.)*

13

SISTER. *(Reading.)* "Versatile easy chair with sleeper incliner, recliner, and swivel rocker mechanism." That's pretty exciting. "Glue blocks, mortise tenon joints and the extensive use of screws instead of staples creates a long-lasting, strong construction."

CARL. Can you beat that?

SISTER. Not with a stick.

CARL. So are we all happy with Furniture World?

BETTY/SISTER. Yes, we are!

CARL. I wanna make both my girls happy. I can't feel good if you're not happy.

BETTY. We're happy, Carl!

SISTER. Happy, happy, happy.

CARL. Well, the deal is set. The deal is made. All the kinks are worked out. What can I tell you? We got the building for a song. I hate to say it, but it was a steal.

BETTY. The owner, he loved you, Carl.

CARL. Paul. Paul Casper. What a swell kid. A real sap but swell.

BETTY. He was impressed with you, Carl. He looked up to you.

CARL. Yeah, yeah. The little puppy's after me to let him be a silent investor in Furniture World. I don't know. Should we let him in? Hey, it's up to you girls.

BETTY. Whatever you think.

CARL. Sister?

SISTER. Do I get a vote?

CARL. You sure do.

SISTER. All right! Well, then ... whatever you think!

CARL. I don't know. I'm not sure. We could use some extra financing. What d'ya say ... What d'ya say we have him over tomorrow night. We could fix cocktails.

BETTY. I'll make one of my hors d'oeuvres trays.

SISTER. I'll make Mother's gingerbread men.

BETTY. Perhaps some canapes.

SISTER. The ones with the raisin eyes.

CARL. Hey, whoa! I'm not saying roll out the red carpet! We don't have to anoint him in oil. Let's just get him over for a drink. We'll sign all the ownership papers and then we'll see do we need a silent partner.

BETTY. Mmm, I like that plan. Kiss me, Daddy.

14

CARL. You got it, Mama. *(They kiss. Sister paces around them.)*

SISTER. Aren't you two a pair of lovebirds. Tweet, tweet, tweet! Grrr! Grrrr! *Tweet!!!*

BETTY. You know what, Carl? I think we should find Sister a man. Sister, wouldn't you be happy if we could find you a man?

SISTER. I don't know. There're so few good ones out there. *(To Carl.)* You're the last of the good catches. After you they broke the mold.

BETTY. Still, I think she could use a man. *(To Carl.)* Wouldn't you feel better if Sister had a man?

CARL. *(A beat.)* The right one though. He'd have to be the right one.

SISTER. *(A beat.)* So you think I need a man?

CARL. It might make you happy.

SISTER. Sure. Yeah. Sure, it would. Hey, how about the man who's coming for cocktails? Would he be my type?

BETTY. Oh, no. I doubt it.

SISTER. Well, maybe you have it figured wrong, my type. See 'cause I like different types. I like all types. With me type doesn't matter.

BETTY. So anyone'll do?

SISTER. Any type'll do. That's different from anyone. I'm not a pushover. In fact, I'm pretty picky. I choose carefully. I like to look at men through a fine-toothed comb. Who knows? Maybe he's the one I've been waiting for all my life. I wouldn't be at all surprised.

CARL. So maybe you should nab him.

SISTER. Then we could have another wedding. We'd all be one big happy family. Running Furniture World, celebrating birthdays, borrowing cups of sugar, lending each other lawn mowers. It could be a very excellent setup. I'm gonna set my cap for him. Do you think that's a good idea? I should set my cap for him?

CARL. Sure.

SISTER. I'll get dolled up. I can look good when I try. It just takes some effort. But the results are something to see. People don't recognize me. They think I'm someone else. They think I'm good-looking. "Hey, Sister, that's not you, is it?" "Sure, it's me. I'm wearing mascara!" I doll up good. I'm a real babe. Shake your boodie.

CARL. Hey, hey! No dirty language. Watch your mouth.

SISTER. Yes, sir, Major Dad! I just got carried away.

CARL. Well, straighten up and fly right.

SISTER. I'm sorry, I just meant — Hey, I can look good.

CARL. Yeah, sure. Maybe Betty can help you.

BETTY. Oh, of course I can. We'll do a complete makeover.

CARL. Now why don't you go out in the yard and shovel up that dog mess.

SISTER. Dog mess? We don't have a dog.

CARL. You don't have to tell me. It's some neighborhood dog. I'm gonna have to poison it. There's no other way. Every morning he leaves a big pile of his mess.

SISTER. Well, I'll take care of it. I'll clean it up.

CARL. That's the spirit. It's good to have you home.

SISTER. It's good to be home. *(Sister goes out into the yard. She picks up a shovel.)*

BETTY. Your sister's weird.

CARL. Yeah, I know.

BETTY. She's got a tattoo. It's like she's some sorta kook.

CARL. She won't be around here forever.

BETTY. Yeah?

CARL. Yeah. *(Betty starts to massage Carl's shoulders. Outside Sister discovers the pile of shit behind a bush.)*

SISTER. Oh, ho! There you are. Holy smoke. That's a big pile all right. *(Sister scoops up the shit, carries it to a garbage can and dumps it. As Betty and Carl continue their conversation in the kitchen, Sister goes up to her room. Up in her room, she takes off her skirt and shoes and sits in her bed-chair wearing her long shirt.)*

BETTY. *(Massaging Carl's shoulders.)* After she signs the papers? Then do you think you can tell her to go?

CARL. Maybe. Probably so. Yeah.

BETTY. Guess what panties I'm wearing?

CARL. Let's see, it's Thursday, right?

BETTY. Uh-huh.

CARL. That's ah, that's … I know! "A bowl of cherries, just 4U."

BETTY. Wrong!

CARL. What?

BETTY. Guess again. *(Betty spins around, her skirt flares out. Carl tries to get a peek at her panties.)*

16

CARL. Lollipop Land?

BETTY. *(Laughing as she continues twirling her skirt.)* That's Wednesday!

CARL. Let me see. *(Carl gets down on all fours.)*

BETTY. It's one of your favorites.

CARL. One of my favorites. *(Betty spins off to the bedroom. Carl follows her on all fours.)* Is it, "Carl's Little Pussy?" I like that one. That's a sweet one. *(The lights slowly change as night begins to fall. Sister sits frozen in the bed-chair in her room.)*

SISTER. *(Spaghetti/Pinkie.)* [SP] I'm sitting here wondering what to do — what to do with the *roast beef* on my chest. A pair of eyes in the beef looking through fat and blood … Gristle is an element; it's part of the deal./ *(She breathes heavily, then speaks in a whisper.)* [P] Maybe you should try and move./ [SP] What?/ [P] You've been sitting here a very long time./ [SP] So?/ [P] Maybe it'd be good to move./ [SP] … Go on then. Be my guest. *(Sister gets out of the bed-chair with some effort, then quickly tiptoes over to the window. A sweet expression illuminates her face.)* [P] Hello. This is my window. I'm trying to learn to fly out of it. I asked for a pair of wings for Christmas. I'll take them in any size, any color. Tell Maw I don't give a damn about the color. But I need a pair that works. Wings that don't work are worse than no wings at all./ [SP] Is that you, Pinkie?/ [P] Yeah. Is that you, Spaghetti?/ [SP] It's me. *(Carl enters the kitchen wearing pajama bottoms. Sister freezes. As Sister.)* Footsteps. *(Carl picks up a big soggy sponge and drains water over his face and neck.)* It's him. He's down there. *(Sister takes off her underpants and comes down the stairs carrying them. She enters the kitchen, Carl looks up at her.)*

CARL. Sister?

SISTER. Yeah. I forgot to wash out my underwear.

CARL. Oh.

SISTER. Why are you still up?

CARL. Can't sleep.

SISTER. Oh.

CARL. I keep thinking this time everything's gotta work out. All the pieces have gotta get in place and stay there. I've had trouble before. But no more. It's too late to fail again. This has got to be my ticket. A cat only has nine lives. It's closing in on me. I'm forty-plus. I look good for my age. No one knows I've had sutures sewn in my head to keep this mop in place. I can dive in a swimming pool. I don't but I could. I don't know. I just feel like I deserve better. I deserve more. When do I get my piece of the pie? I don't want dog scraps. Where's my roast beef?

SISTER. *(After a beat.)* Don't worry, Carl. I'll help you get your roast beef.

CARL. *(Near tears.)* You will?

SISTER. Sure.

CARL. That's my girl. There's no one I can love any more than you.

SISTER. Yes, and there's no one I can love any more than you.

CARL. I know that. In my heart I know that.

SISTER. Carl. I got something for you. *(Sister gets a bowl.)*

CARL. What? I don't deserve anything. I don't deserve a thing. I never have. *(Sister presents the bowl to Carl.)*

SISTER. M&Ms. All the red ones. I saved all the red ones for you.

CARL. Well, look at that. That's very thoughtful. *(A beat.)* Would you … Would you feed them to me?

SISTER. *(A beat.)* Sure, Carl. *(Sister picks up a handful of the red M&Ms. She feeds them to Carl one by one. Carl eats them slowly at first, then he eats them faster and faster. Finally, he is licking them out of the palm of her hand. Betty enters in a negligee.)*

BETTY. Carl.

CARL. I couldn't sleep. I was hungry. She fixed me some M&Ms.

BETTY. How sweet of her. Do you want me to fix you a shake?

CARL. Yes, I do.

BETTY. I will then. What's this in the sink? *(Betty picks up Sister's soaking wet underpants.)*

SISTER. Those are mine. I'll take them. I have to hang them out to dry. *(Sister takes the underpants, twists and shakes them, then goes to the backyard.)*

BETTY. Did you see that? She shook water at me. I don't like this; she gives me the creeps. Washing her personal items in our kitchen sink. Look at that ring. Where's my Ajax? *(Betty starts cleaning the kitchen sink. In the yard Sister hangs her underpants out to dry, then goes upstairs to her bedroom.)* This has got to be spotless. We want our porcelain to sparkle. Everything has got to stay sanitized! *(Pleading to Carl.)* Won't you please help me?!

CARL. Sure, Baby, sure. I'll help you. I'll protect you. I'm your man. Didn't I save you once already?

BETTY. Yeah. Me and my Christmas tree.

CARL. You and your Christmas tree, that's right.

BETTY. It's just — everything was going just right and then she had to come into the picture.

CARL. Look, as soon as she signs the papers —

BETTY. Tomorrow night, right?

CARL. Yeah. Paul Casper's coming at six P.M. He'll be here with the papers.

BETTY. Good.

CARL. Who knows — maybe that sap'll take her off our hands. He's not married or encumbered. Maybe he'll want her.

BETTY. *(Shaking her head.)* That guy's bad news. He's got problems. Severe problems.

CARL. Like what?

BETTY. Nothing. Just some things I observed while you were off checking the plumbing in the ladies.

CARL. What things?

BETTY. I don't want you getting mad at me. None of it is my fault.

CARL. Hey, don't you know, I know nothing could ever be your fault?

BETTY. *(A beat.)* Well, when we were standing there in the warehouse, he started looking at me.

CARL. Yeah? He looked at you? Well, you're good to look at. I guess he couldn't help himself. That's something I can understand.

BETTY. He took off his jacket and stretched his arms above his head. There were big sweat marks underneath his arms.

CARL. Kid's got no manners. Maybe I should teach him some manners.

BETTY. He said I got him hot. Looking at me got him hot. He said would I —

CARL. Yeah?

BETTY. "Suck him dry."

CARL. Oh no.

BETTY. "Suck me dry. Make me cry like a baby. Like a little baby. I wanna come through your nose."

19

CARL. This — What? This is … My God. I'm sick. I'm sick. *(Carl is secretly turned on.)* I'll kill him. I — I'll kill him.

BETTY. Carl, no.

CARL. I will. I'll smash — I'll rip — I'll murder. That's right, I'll murder him.

BETTY. Murder? You would murder him for me?

CARL. Yes.

BETTY. Oh, God. Oh, Carl. When?

CARL. I don't know. Soon.

BETTY. Tomorrow night?

CARL. Right. Yes. That'll be the time. That's when.

BETTY. Do you think it'll be before or after hors d'oeuvres?

CARL. I don't know.

BETTY. I'm wondering for shopping purposes.

CARL. I don't know. Whatever seems right.

BETTY. I'll cook in case.

CARL. God. This was gonna be good. Things were gonna be different. We were making improvements. Now I have to murder this — this slime. Oh God. It just makes me sick.

BETTY. Oh, it makes me sick too. It does. It does. Maybe you shouldn't do it.

CARL. What? I should just go on and go ahead with the deal? Include him in as a silent partner?

BETTY. Yeah.

CARL. But he insulted you.

BETTY. It wasn't the worst I ever —

CARL. Worse what, you ever what? What?

BETTY. *(A whisper.)* Swallowed.

CARL. God. You … You did it then?

BETTY. For you. I did it for you. So you could be somebody.

CARL. God — This — God — No. This — really, Betty. This is not how I get to be somebody. Wrong. We are thinking wrong here and now I have to commit murder. Otherwise, I have no dignity. No human dignity. No right to walk upright. I'd have to regress to all fours.

BETTY. But he was going to be our main investor.

CARL. I know that. And it's too bad but he dies. As soon as he signs the bill of sale, he's gone.

BETTY. You do love me.

CARL. Yes.

BETTY. Show me how.

CARL. No. I can't. I have to kill him first. Then you'll be pure again and you'll respect me all the more because I took care of you. I took a stand. A respectable stand.

BETTY. Oh, Carl, you're such a good strong man.

CARL. Yeah? Well, how 'bout you fix me that shake now. You know just how I like it. *(Betty turns on the shake machine. Sounds of loud, violent lovemaking mixed with the sick sounds of deranged people laughing and screaming on a roller coaster come from the machine. Sister sits up in the bed-chair, waken from a terrible dream.)*

SISTER. *(Sister/Spaghetti/Pinkie.)*

[SIS] Where's my face? Where's my face? What have they done with my face? I can't stand around here without a face that is not going to work, everything must work, let it work out. Please, I am begging you. Drench, drench. "Can't you straighten up and fly right?!" Fly — fly —/ *(Sister races to the window. The noise from the shake machine stops.)* [SP] I fell out a window. I fell out a window. I wanted to fall and crack open my skull./ [P] What would be inside? Oh, such surprises: tangerines, necklaces that sparkle, gold teeth, fine ribbon, chocolate wrapped in red foil. All my brains are treasures. How wonderful what I see. I could weep with joy. Rainbow tears drift from the window. It's an outrage. Who will catch the tears? No one is below; I am crying colored tears and no one is below. *(The lights dim to black, then slowly brighten to a pink-gold sunrise. We hear the sound of birds chirping. Carl enters the kitchen from his bedroom, then moves out into the yard. He wears his pajama bottoms. Sister sleeps at the window. Carl looks up at her, sees she is sleeping then squats behind a bush and takes a big shit in the yard. He gets up and exits to his bedroom. Sister sniffs and sniffs again.)* [P] I smell something. Something bad./ [SP] You don't./ [P] I can't help it, I do. I have to tell the truth. To thine own self be true./ [SP] I don't think so./ [P] I do./ [SP] Yeah? Well, you've never once gotten up and braved the light of day without lying your whole heart out. You tell yourself, I'm not gonna die; what I do is important; my life is good; I'm gonna have a nice day. Ah, ah, ah! That's better. Now I can rise to my feet soaked in the cum of canards and meet the day. Hello, day! Tweet, tweet. The birdies are chirping./ [P] Ooh, aren't those baby birdies sweet?!/ [SP] I'd like to snap their scrawny necks. *(Sister puts on her skirt and shoes. She takes off the wig she is wearing and puts on a different one. We see she is nearly bald with horrible little bloody tufts sticking out all over her head. Betty enters the kitchen humming. She is dressed in the same outfit she wore yesterday. She pours a liquid mixture into a frying pan. Carl enters wearing the same suit he wore in the first scene.)*

CARL. Good morning, Honey.

BETTY. Good morning, Sweetie.

CARL. What's for breakfast?

BETTY. Bubbles.

CARL. Mmm, my favorite.

BETTY. Goodie. Oh, Carl?

CARL. Yeah?

BETTY. I'm thinking we shouldn't mention anything to Sister about …

CARL. What?

BETTY. Our plans for the guest.

CARL. No, no. Absolutely. Let's keep that under our hats.

BETTY. Right. Just act natural.

CARL. Yeah. Like any other day. *(Sister comes down the stairs.)*

SISTER. Good morning, world!

CARL. Good morning, Sister.

BETTY. Nice day. Carl, are you ready for your bubbles?

CARL. You bet. *(Betty blows bubbles from the liquid in the frying pan. She blows the bubbles over to Carl who pokes at them with his fork and gobbles them up.)* Mmm. Scrumptious. So light. They just melt in my mouth.

SISTER. I thought you never ate breakfast.

CARL. I'm a changed man.

SISTER. Mother would never believe this. Carly eating a big wholesome breakfast. Breakfast was not his bag.

CARL. *(Wiping his lips.)* Goodness! I'm stuffed!

BETTY. Breakfast is the most important meal of the day. It's full of nutrients. Now, everyone, I'm making out a shopping list. Does anyone need anything from the market?

SISTER. Yes, I do. I'm making gingerbread men to serve our

22

guest this evening. They were Mother's specialty.

BETTY. Oh. Well, I'm sure our guest will be delighted. What ingredients do you need?

SISTER. Let's see ... Gingerbread mix. Oh, and raisins. Don't forget the raisins. Mother always used the raisins for their eyes. *(To Carl.)* Remember how she'd let us help her put them in? *(Pretending to put raisins in the eyes of gingerbread men.)* Bing. Bing.

CARL. She didn't like it if you ate the raisins.

SISTER. No, but if one fell on the floor, you could have it.

CARL. It had to be an accident. I mean you couldn't just start throwing raisins on the floor. It had to be an accident. Then you could eat it. Other than that, you'd have to wait till the men were cooked and then you could eat out their raisin eyes.

BETTY. I never thought much of raisins. I have no real use for them.

SISTER. Good! More raisins for us!

BETTY. Well, I'm off to the market. I'll be back shortly.

SISTER. Oh, and maybe you should pick up some red glitter. After we sign the papers it'd be fun to throw up some big handfuls of glitter. *(She mimes throwing up big handfuls of glitter and watching it fall.)* Yo! Yo! Whoosh!

BETTY. I — well — excuse me — But I have an opinion here. Carl?

CARL. Yes, Betty, what's your opinion?

BETTY. Glitter makes too big a mess. It's sort of pretty for one second, then there's this big mess.

SISTER. I'll clean it up.

BETTY. That's impossible. You can never clean up all the glitter. You'll always be finding it in shoes and corners for years and years to come. It's a great big mess. I vote no on the glitter.

SISTER. I vote *yes.*

BETTY. Carl?

CARL. *(A beat.)* I think maybe we should ... table the issue.

BETTY. *(A beat.)* I don't understand. I thought you wanted a lovely home? This can never be a lovely home with cheap, filthy glitter sticking up under our sink, gummed all up our air vents.

CARL. All right. No glitter. It's too big a mess. We can't have it.

SISTER. I want glitter!

23

CARL. I said, No! Look, we have to have rules. Sometimes it's very good to have boundaries. Free rein'll freeze you. Ya gotta put a man on a path to make him happy.

BETTY. That is so true. That is a truth. You know what, Carl? If you ever get tired of the furniture business, you should become a philosopher. You could write a hit book in a minute. *(Carl blushes. Betty pecks him on the cheek, then hands Sister a basket.)* Oh, Sister, would you go out in the garden this morning and pick some fresh vegetables? We'll have a garden salad with dinner. It's full of nutrients. *(Betty exits humming.)*

SISTER. Where're my cats? I haven't seen my cats.

CARL. She's allergic to cats. I put them in a cage. They're out in the backyard.

SISTER. You don't put cats in cages. Cages are for chickens or rabbits or hamsters. They don't even make cat cages.

CARL. You're getting an attitude. Don't get an attitude. *(A beat.)* I gotta go get some poison. Tonight I'm gonna get rid of that neighborhood dog. *(Carl goes into the yard. Sister follows him outside carrying the basket.)*

SISTER. I don't think she's gonna fit in around here. She doesn't even like raisins.

CARL. Hey, maybe you're still young or something. Maybe you've never stopped to think about *my* needs. But I do have a few. Aren't I allowed to have just a few? *(Sister kneels on the ground and starts pulling up vegetables.)* Try to understand. I need a homemaker. Someone to care for me. To make things cozy. She feeds me meals; she waxes the floor. She wears a different colored negligee each night of the week. She sews dainty little writing on her panties. It reads, "Carl's Girl," or "Carl's Little Pussy." I think that stuff is cute. Nobody's ever done that sort of thing for me.

SISTER. *(Pulling up vegetables.)* So you've found yourself a mate. I'm very happy for you. I just hope it doesn't end in cheap divorce or desertion like your last three marriages.

CARL. *(A beat.)* You know what's going on with you? I'm starting to get it now. It's starting to make itself clear. You're jealous.

SISTER. What?

CARL. I think you're just plain jealous.

SISTER. Don't say that.

24

CARL. Jealous 'cause you can't get a man. You can't get a man.
SISTER. Hey, look, I don't care. You wanna fuck her? Stick these carrots up every place in her; make her scream like a pig? Fine! *(She breaks carrots in two and throws them at him.)* Fine! Save the carrots! I'll cook them up for dinner and serve them with butter. I'll eat a big serving of them! I'll ask for seconds! That's how jealous I am, you rotten fucking failure!!!
CARL. *(A beat.)* Pick up those carrots. Pick them up. All of them. Now. *(She slowly crawls on her knees and starts picking up broken carrots.)*
SISTER. I'm sorry, Carl. I didn't mean to — I'm sorry —
CARL. Don't talk. I oughtta rip your head off your shoulders. Did you get all the carrots? *(She nods her head, her fists full of broken carrots.)* I don't think you did. *(Carl picks up a dirty, broken carrot, takes it to her and jams it in her mouth. Carl walks out of the yard, leaving Sister kneeling in the dirt. Sister crawls to the basket and drops the carrots into the basket.)*
SISTER. *(Spaghetti/Pinkie.)* [SP] I gotta be careful. I gotta watch my mouth. Speaking in evil./ *(She slaps herself.)* [P] Don't hit me!/ [SP] Shut up! I will if I want to!/ *(She slaps herself and pulls at her hair.)* [P] Ow! Ow! Ow! Stop it! You're hurting me./ [SP] Then, shut up. *(She stops beating herself and sighs with exhaustion — as Sister.)* Oh goodness. Goodness. *(Tiptoeing around the yard.)* I don't know who I am anymore. There's this real sense I am lost. I have gotten lost. The path has disappeared and the berries have been eaten by the wren. I'm out here all alone and I can't even call because I don't know what name to call. Who would come and get me? What if I called for them and I called and then I was forsaken. *(The shrieking sound of cats howling blares across the sky.)* [SIS] My cats! Where are you? I hear you. Garfield? Plums? *(Sister discovers her two fat cats crammed in a tiny cage hidden between the bushes.)* Oh, there you are! Why, they've caged you up. Put you in a cage. Not to worry. Cages can be good. You have bars. Something to hold on to. Solid. You're not lost. You're there in the cage. People can watch you. But they can't touch. They may throw peanuts. Peanuts can hurt. But they can't kill. If you're in the cage. Good kitties. Good kitties. *(Sister returns the cats and goes to check her soggy underpants.)* Still wet. Dripping wet. I can't wear pants that are this wet. Dry,

will you. (*Sister heads up to her room through the outdoor stairway.*) I gotta doll up. I'm setting my cap for the guest. Carl'll be proud of me. He'll see I'm really good-looking. He'll see I can get a man. (*Sister enters her bedroom, then exits into her bathroom. Betty enters the kitchen from the carport door, carrying a sack of groceries. She starts taking the groceries out of the sack. The "groceries" are all identical cans of string beans. She puts the cans in various places as though each can were a different item. Paul Casper, twenties-thirties, enters. He is thin and wiry with a broken nose. He wears a silver necklace and a dagger earring.*)

PAUL. Hello, Mrs. Willard.

BETTY. What do you want?

PAUL. … More.

BETTY. Get out of here.

PAUL. I thought you invited me.

BETTY. Later. That's for later. You're supposed to come here later.

PAUL. I wanna come now.

BETTY. No. Go away. Later you can come back by. We're having cocktails and hors d'oeuvres. But I have to prepare all that. I have to do the preparation.

PAUL. Let me help.

BETTY. It's woman's work. You'd be in the way.

PAUL. That's where I wanna be — in your way.

BETTY. I don't think Carl would like this. You talking to me this way.

PAUL. I don't think Carl would like how you talked to me on top of the coffee table.

BETTY. I don't remember saying anything.

PAUL. You don't? That's funny.

BETTY. I'd like for you to leave.

PAUL. You told me you wanted to suck me dry. You said you wanted to make me cry like a little baby. You said you wanted me to come through your nose.

BETTY. … I didn't mean it.

PAUL. What? You didn't mean what?

BETTY. Anything I said or did.

PAUL. It felt like you meant it. It felt exactly like you meant it. It felt like you lost control.

26

BETTY. No. I was acting. It was all an act.

PAUL. I don't believe you.

BETTY. I just did it so you'd give Carl a good price on the building.

PAUL. Yeah?

BETTY. Yeah.

PAUL. I don't believe you.

BETTY. Why not? It worked, didn't it? You're selling the place to him for peanuts.

PAUL. Yeah. That's true. I am. But that's 'cause I want to get rid of it. I want someone to take it off my hands.

BETTY. Why's that?

PAUL. I got the word. Some ponies I owe are gonna explode it on Sunday.

BETTY. So you're selling Carl a building that's gonna be blown up?

PAUL. Kaboom.

BETTY. Why are you telling me this?

PAUL. 'Cause I don't want you to be there. I want you to be with me.

BETTY. I just told you everything I said or did was for Carl.

PAUL. And I think I mentioned, I don't believe you.

BETTY. I love Carl. Carl loves me. We have a lovely home.

PAUL. Uh-huh.

BETTY. You don't believe me, but Carl would do anything for me.

PAUL. You're nothing but an ornament to Carl. He only wants the deodorized airbrushed version of you. I want all of you. Every sweet dirty part. Naked under fluorescent lights. I crave all your wrinkles and bags and ugly lies. I never ever want to fuck you in the moonlight.

BETTY. *(A beat.)* Carl's going to murder you. Tonight when you come over. He's making plans to kill you.

PAUL. Why?

BETTY. You insulted me.

PAUL. Did you tell him I did?

BETTY. Yes.

PAUL. Why did you tell him that?

BETTY. I don't know. I wanted to see — I wanted to know — I wanted proof — he loved me.

PAUL. He doesn't love you. He's too stupid to love you. He doesn't even know you were a whore and burnt apartment buildings for money and drowned your son in a bucket.

BETTY. *(Weakly, staggered.)* How do you know that was me?

PAUL. I'm looking at your face.

BETTY. *(A beat.)* I never should have married Carl. He's not for me. I think I was desperate. It was Christmas Eve. I was being evicted. I tried to get the money. That night I went to the Pleasure Chest. I bought some rubber gloves and condoms. I jerked two guys off in the parking lot. Neither of them paid me. I went back to my apartment and sat down in the corner of the green couch wearing my coat. I sat there the longest time in my coat. The sun came up. I wanted to cook eggs. I wanted eggs and hot coffee. But I just sat there and then night fell. The following morning I was still there in the coat. The doorbell rang; it was Carl coming by for his cold reading class. I told him things weren't so good. I told him I was in a bad way. He took me out to McDonald's and he bought me an Egg McMuffin. It was congealed and cold. I ate it. Then I fucked him. We went back to the apartment. It was padlocked. My things had been put out in the yard. I got some stuff: clothes; a hair dryer; the Christmas tree; and then I moved in here and tried to make it work.

PAUL. Let's kill Carl.

BETTY. Really?

PAUL. I think so.

BETTY. Can't we just run away?

PAUL. Don't you want his money?

BETTY. He doesn't have any money. His mother left it all to his screwed-up sister.

PAUL. But he's buying my building.

BETTY. Only with her signature.

PAUL. Hmm.

BETTY. After he pays you for the building, we'll have half the money.

PAUL. Right. But wouldn't it be better if we had all the money? Maybe I could marry the sister and then kill her.

BETTY. I wouldn't mind seeing her dead. As a matter of fact, she's setting her cap for you.

PAUL. Yeah?

BETTY. She's trying to find a man.

28

PAUL. Great. Make me look good to her. Build me up. Can you do that, baby?

BETTY. Yeah. I can do that. *(Carl enters the yard. He carries a brown sack. He is singing "When Johnny Comes Marching Home Again")* There's Carl — You gotta go.

PAUL. Hey, whatta ya say we kill him just once for good measure?

BETTY. Yeah, maybe, yeah.

PAUL. Give me some of you. I want some of you before I go. *(Betty sticks her hand up between her legs. She gasps, then holds her wet fingers out to Paul. He grabs her hand and smears her scent across his lips and nose. Carl enters just as Paul exits.)*

CARL. I got the poison.

BETTY. Poison?

CARL. I thought it'd be a good way to go. You know, with our guest.

BETTY. Oh yes. But, well, I — I'm having second thoughts.

CARL. Sure you are. You're a woman. This is man's work. Relax, let me take charge.

BETTY. But, I mean, it's just ... I don't ... Isn't Sister setting her cap for this guy?

CARL. *(Ominously.)* Sister better watch her step if she knows what's good for her. If she doesn't straighten up and fly right, she could be next. *(Taking a can of poison from the sack.)* I got plenty of pest control. For anyone who gets pesty. *(The lights dim down below and go up on Sister's room. Sister enters from her bathroom. She has on a blonde wig with ringlets. She wears a bra and petticoat, high heels and dangling earrings. She carries a pink evening dress with a full net skirt. She holds the dress up to her body and parades around the room.)*

SISTER. *(Spaghetti/Pinkie.)* [SIS] How to get a man! How to catch a man. How to reel one in. That is the question./ [P] Well, it certainly helps being a virgin./ [SP] A virgin? Are you a virgin?/ [P] I think I'm a virgin./ [SP] I'm not so sure you are./ [P] Oh really?/ [SP] I have my doubts./ [P] I hope you're right./ [SP] I thought you liked being a virgin./ [P] There's always this fear./ [SP] Fear?/ [P] Of the unknown. *(Pulling at her bangs.)* [P] I don't like these bangs./ [SP] No. *(Sister rips off her bangs. She tosses them out the window just as Betty enters her room after a perfunctory knock.)*

BETTY. Hello.

SISTER. Hi.

BETTY. I — thought you might want some help.

SISTER. Help?

BETTY. I thought maybe I could give you some tips on how to set your cap for our guest.

SISTER. Tips? I need tips?

BETTY. Maybe. I don't know. Do you date around much?

SISTER. I like to keep love at bay.

BETTY. Why's that?

SISTER. You know what they say: Only love can break your heart.

BETTY. Did someone break your heart?

SISTER. Once. But I got this tattoo to forget him by.

BETTY. What is it?

SISTER. A face with no eyes surrounded by a cracked heart.

BETTY. Did it hurt?

SISTER. No. It felt good. What tips do you know?

BETTY. *(A beat.)* First thing is don't be overeager. Never say nice things to him. Curb that impulse. Tell him he makes your skin crawl. Tell him to stay away. Tell him the mere sight of him makes you wanna carve out your eyes. You know, play hard to get.

SISTER. Right. Play hard to get. They give that advice in magazines.

BETTY. Yeah, exactly. So what're ya gonna say if he proposes?

SISTER. Proposes? You mean marriage?

BETTY. Yeah.

SISTER. I'll say sure! Thanks! I do! I do! Now kiss the bride! *(She makes smacking sounds with her lips.)*

BETTY. Wait a minute. Think about it. You're not playing hard to get.

SISTER. But he wants to marry me. He wants me to be his bride!

BETTY. Oh no, not really. He's testing you. He wants to find out if you're easy. If you're a slut, a tramp, a whore. No nice girl ever says yes to a first-time marriage proposal.

SISTER. Gosh, I don't know. I think about it and it'd be hard to keep saying, "No." I mean I never ever remember even once saying, "No," and I'm speaking of my whole life.

BETTY. Well, go ahead then, be my guest. He'll end up tossing you away like a piece of unfinished toast.

SISTER. Toast?

BETTY. Yeah.

30

SISTER. Well, I hope he doesn't do that. I'm not toast. I'm better than toast.

BETTY. Then play hard to get. No matter what he says, say, "No." Always "no." Keep telling him "no, no, no!"

SISTER. "No." I'll tell him "No." Now I better check on my gingerbread men.

BETTY. I'll take them out for you. You fix your earrings. You've got them on backwards.

SISTER. Oh! *(Betty exits. Sister turns to Spaghetti/Pinkie.)* [P] So there, you see, all you have to do is say the magic word — "No" — and he won't think you're less than toast./ [SP] But I am less than toast./ [P] Ssh, they don't have to know./ [SP] Oh, they'll know. They'll spot it right off. You'll never pass the mustard./ [P] I won't?/ [SP] No way. Come on, let's get while the getting's good./ [P] Where?/ [SP] Out the window. *(Sister goes to the window and hangs the pink dress outside.)* [SP] Now jump. Go on, jump./ [P] Wait, I need my wings. Without wings I will die./ [SP] Yes, but before you'll be sailing through the air like glitter./ [P] But that'll go so fast and then I'll be smashed./ [SP] Not while you're in the air. In the air every second is forever. Now fly. Just fly. Fly, fly, fly! *(Sister sails her dress out the window. Paul appears in the yard. He sees the falling dress and catches it in his arms.)*

PAUL. Whoa! Whoa! *(Speaking to the dress.)* How do you do? So nice to meet you. Shall we dance? *(Paul waltzes the dress around the yard, singing a song.)* Mmm. The way you move. I feel like I've known you all my life. Will you marry me?

SISTER. *(Yelling down from her window.)* Hey, that's my one fancy dress and I don't know if I can let you marry it.

PAUL. Why, hello there.

SISTER. Hi.

PAUL. Did you really think I wanted to marry this dress?

SISTER. I don't know. You asked it.

PAUL. I was being playful.

SISTER. Oh. Playful.

PAUL. Do you know who I really want to marry? *(Sister shakes her head.)* The girl who fits into this dress. That's the girl for me.

SISTER. Well, I — I mean, it's my dress.

PAUL. Yes. I believe you. I have no doubt. Would you do me a favor and come step into your gown?

SISTER. All right. *(Sister comes down the outdoor stairway.)*

PAUL. What's your name?

SISTER. Sister Willard.

PAUL. Nice to meet you, Sister. I'm Paul Casper.

SISTER. You're the guest.

PAUL. Yes. *(Paul helps Sister into her dress. It is a perfect fit.)* Beautiful. Just beautiful. *(Sister turns around.)* Breathlessly beautiful. *(Dropping to his knees.)* Sister Willard, will you please marry me?

SISTER. I — I — I — I — *(Sister timidly shakes her head back and forth.)*

PAUL. What?

SISTER. *(Shaking her head.)* Uh-uh.

PAUL. Was that yes?

SISTER. *(A whisper.)* No.

PAUL. No?

SISTER. No.

PAUL. *(Approaching her.)* But I — I love you, Sister Willard. I love you more than words can say.

SISTER. No. Stay away.

PAUL. I can't. I could never stay away. Not from your lips, your hair, your tattoo.

SISTER. I said, No. No. The mere sight of you makes me want to scoop out my eyeballs.

PAUL. For God's sake. I'll — I'll have plastic surgery. I'll change my face, my voice, my sex! Anything! Anything for you.

SISTER. No.

PAUL. I won't take no for an answer.

SISTER. No, no, no, no, no.

PAUL. Yes.

SISTER. No!

PAUL. Oooh. I really like it when you tell me no. It's starting to get me hot. Tell me no some more. Please, tell me some more.

SISTER. No.

PAUL. Yes.

SISTER. No, no, no! Ten thousand times no!

PAUL. Yes, yes — I want it.

SISTER. No, no, no —

PAUL. Yes!

SISTER. No. Oooh. *(Sister starts having spontaneous orgasms all across the yard.)*

PAUL. Come on, baby.

SISTER. Ooh! Ooh!

PAUL. More, I want more!

SISTER. No! No! A zillion times, no!

PAUL. Yes! Oh, yes!

SISTER. Ooh! Ooh!

PAUL. Take it.

SISTER. No; no; no; no.

PAUL. Yes, yes.

SISTER. Oooh! OOOh! OOOOOH! OOOOOOOHH! *(Sister collapses to the ground exhausted and panting. Paul produces a giant engagement ring.)*

PAUL. I'm gonna ask you just one more time. Sister Willard, will you marry me?

SISTER. I — I — I — *(Convulsing with orgasms all alone on the ground.)* OOh! OOH! OOOHH!

PAUL. You will?

SISTER. *(Weakly.)* Yes. *(Paul puts the ring on her finger. Betty enters the kitchen from her bedroom. She wears a frilly apron over her dress. Carl enters.)*

BETTY. It's party time! *(Betty takes a plate of canapes out of the refrigerator.)*

CARL. Yes. It'll all go off without a hitch. Smooth as glass. There's no need for concern of any sort.

BETTY. I'll take out the hors d'oeuvres.

CARL. Yes, I'll turn on the Malibu lights. *(Betty and Carl enter the yard and discover Sister and Paul lying on the lawn side by side.)*

BETTY. Well, look who's here.

CARL. What's going on?

SISTER. *(Showing her ring.)* We're engaged, Carl. We're getting married. I got a man.

CARL. What do you mean? You don't even know this punk.

PAUL. I'm afraid it was love at first sight. At least for me. Sister had some initial hesitation, but I finally was able to win her over.

SISTER. It wasn't easy. Was it, Paul?

33

PAUL. Not in the least.

SISTER. I must have told him "No" over a zillion times.

PAUL. But when she at last said "Yes," I sensed she meant it.

SISTER. Aren't you happy, Carl? Aren't you happy for me?

CARL. *(To Paul.)* Get outta here.

PAUL. What?

CARL. I said get outta here before I break your face.

BETTY. Carl —

PAUL. Look, Carl, don't be a hothead. Relax.

CARL. You relax this — *(Carl hits Paul.)*

BETTY/SISTER. Carl!

PAUL. Hey, man?! What's your beef?

CARL. What's my beef? I don't have any beef. All I get are dog scraps! *(Carl swings at Paul again. Paul comes back at Carl. They tear into each other. Paul quickly gets the upper hand and starts pummeling Carl. The women come in and break them up.)*

BETTY. Will you knock it off. Stop it. Come on!

SISTER. *(Overlapping.)* Don't! Stop! Don't! You're hurting him! Stop, please. You don't have to kill him!

PAUL. He's stupid, your brother!

SISTER. He just lost control or something. Usually he's really nice. He's a nice guy.

BETTY. *(To Carl.)* Carl! Hey, hey! Carl, what're you doing? You're supposed to kill him in an orderly fashion after the papers are signed.

CARL. Right. Right. I lost my head.

BETTY. Whoa! That was a good one! Let's give him a hand! *(She starts clapping.)* My star pupil! Acting is believing! I'm telling you, this man could be one of the great screen actors of our generation. He claims he's too old to break into the biz. He sees his age as a limitation. But I tell him, "Hollywood loves newcomers. They snarf them up. Go ahead. Do yourself a favor. Be the flavor of the month." But he says, "Nay, I'll stick to furniture." But he has it. He has got it. The potential. Major potential. In all my years as a cold reading coach, I've never seen such a bundle of it.

SISTER. *(To Carl.)* You mean you weren't really mad?

CARL. No. What? Hey! I was acting. This is great. Someone's finally taking my little sister off my hands. After all these years, she's finally found a man. Me and Mother never thought it was

34

possible. *(A beat.)* So! How 'bout we go on and sign those papers, then eat some of Betty's hors d'oeuvres and have a little toast.

PAUL. *(Producing the papers.)* Yes! Those papers. I have them. They're right here. Ta-da! *(Fumbling for a pen.)* Now where's a — *(Betty and Carl both produce pens.)*

BETTY/CARL. Here, here.

PAUL. Got one, thanks. *(Paul quickly signs the papers, then hands them to Carl.)* There you go.

CARL. Now, Sister, I believe we need your John Hancock. *(Carl hands Sister the papers and a pen.)* Right on the dotted line.

SISTER. What am I signing?

CARL. What do you mean "What am I signing?" You're signing a paper I'm telling you to sign. *(Sister reads over the contract.)* What's this? Malcolm Forbes Jr. we got here? Go on already. Sign it.

SISTER. … No.

CARL. What?

SISTER. If I'm marrying Paul, why should I buy his building? I mean shouldn't we just share and share alike? *(Everyone laughs politely at her.)*

CARL. No, no, no. Excuse me, Paul. She doesn't have a head for business. Let me explain. I'll make it extremely simple. You have to sign the paper so I can open up Furniture World.

SISTER. *(A beat.)* But I wanna spend the money Mother left me to open up a Frosty Shop. I want to experiment with all the frozen delights.

CARL. Hey, what're you doing here? You want me to knock your head off your shoulders?

SISTER. No.

CARL. Then sign the paper.

SISTER. *(Reckless and sexy.)* No, no, no, no, no, no, no! God, that's fun! Now I believe I'll go bring out the gingerbread men for our guest. They're my specialty! *(Sister exits into the kitchen.)*

CARL. Did you see that? Did you see that? How am I supposed to handle that and not break open her face?

BETTY. Your sister's weird. *(In the kitchen Sister opens the oven and discovers the gingerbread men are burnt. She quickly pulls the tray of men out of the oven, burns her hand, and drops the tray onto the floor. All the burnt men shatter.)*

SISTER. Ooh! They're all burnt! Oh no! Oh no! They're all broken. My little men! *(She kneels down among the black, broken gingerbread men and tries to piece them back together.)* Broken! Burnt, black, and charred. All in pieces with melted eyes. *(Outside everyone has heard Sister's wailing. Carl shakes his head.)*

CARL. I don't know what's going on here. Maybe she's got the PMS disease. Women. Can they make you sick or what? *(Betty begins passing out hors d'oeuvres.)*

BETTY. Hors d'oeuvres?

CARL. I mean what makes them so special? All that equipment they're always lugging around. Making such a big deal out of having babies. Bearing brats. Think about it. Dogs, cats, mules, cows — you don't see them getting morning sickness. Why's that? Answer's simple. It's something "women" make up 'cause they're just too prissy to live.

BETTY. *(To Carl.)* Try a tuna spread, honey.

CARL. No — I — I think it's time for a toast. I think we all could use a little toast. *(Carl goes into the kitchen. As soon as he is out of sight, Paul and Betty leap on each other. They roll out of sight behind trees and bushes. In the kitchen Carl discovers Sister kneeling among the gingerbread men, trying to piece the charred crumbs together.)*

SISTER. I can't make them fit. Nothing will fit. It's all pieces. Not one man survived.

CARL. Throw that away. Put it in the garbage.

SISTER. Away. I'll throw them away. Away. Like unfinished toast. *(Sister throws the burnt men into the garbage. Throughout the following, Carl sets a tray with four glasses on the kitchen table.)* Carl.

CARL. What?

SISTER. Why aren't you hitting me?

CARL. I'm taking into consideration your extenuating circumstances.

SISTER. What circumstances?

CARL. You have woman problems. But I'm going to fix you a nice drink. After you drink it, you'll feel a whole lot better. Now go wash off those burnt crumbs. Make yourself decent.

SISTER. Decent. Right. Decent. *(Sister goes up to her room and exits into the bathroom. Carl opens up a bottle of blue wine and starts pouring blue wine into glasses. Outside, Betty and Paul reappear extremely disheveled. They quickly try to regain control.)*

PAUL. God, I'm addicted to you before we even start.

BETTY. Are we gonna kill Carl?

PAUL. What do you think?

BETTY. Kill him. I hate him.

PAUL. All right. I'll have to make it look good though, so Sister won't get suspicious. So she'll still marry me.

BETTY. I don't want you marrying her. Let's run away.

PAUL. We need money. After they blow up my building, I got nothing.

BETTY. I can always turn some tricks.

PAUL. Face it, those days are gone.

BETTY. What do you mean they're gone? I thought you wanted to fuck me under fluorescents?

PAUL. Yeah, but baby, I'm in love with you. I'm not fucking your body. I'm fucking your soul.

BETTY. I think my soul's been fucked enough.

PAUL. Hey, you know what I'm saying. I only have eyes for you.

BETTY. Yeah?

PAUL. Yeah. When I think of you I get butterflies in my stomach, those old-fashioned kind. The tiny yellow and white kind. The kind that tickle. Remember them?

BETTY. Yeah. Maybe.

PAUL. So how's Carl planning to kill me?

BETTY. Poison. But don't worry. Don't sweat. I got it figured. I'm going in and doing the old switcheroo-with-the-glasses number. That'll put a fly in his ointment.

PAUL. Aren't you the cagey one.

BETTY. Grrr. *(Paul drops to his knees in front of Betty. He starts slowly kissing and licking her from her ankles to her thighs. Sister enters her bedroom from the bathroom. She waves three burning cigarettes.)*

SISTER. *(Pinkie/Spaghetti.)* [P] Has someone been smoking up here? Remember this is a smoke-free house. No smoking allowed. *(Sister opens a drawer that is overflowing with cigarette stubs. She sticks the cigarettes into the mound of gray ashes.)* Good. Good. Now you're good except for the cookies./ [SP] Ssh. They don't have to know the cookies crumbled. Keep it under your hair. *(She feels up under her wig — as Sister.)* Ooh! Umph! These ringlets aren't you.

They're not close. Not by a good measure. *(Sister takes off her wig and looks for another one.)* Let's see … There must be another one — a someone here — who could be you. Come out, come out, wherever you are … *(Sister hears soft moans coming from the yard below. She moves to the window and looks down. In the yard, Paul is still sucking on Betty. Her moans intensify, then they subside. Betty and Paul break away from each other. Betty straightens her apron and moves into the kitchen. Sister stands still for a moment staring down at Paul, then exits into her bathroom. Betty enters the kitchen. Carl has the blue wine poured.)*

BETTY. You need any help? *(Carl takes a poison pellet from the box.)*

CARL. This one's for our guest. *(Carl ritualistically drops the pellet into a glass. The blue wine fizzles and green vapors appear.)* And this one's for our little Sister. *(Carl drops a second pellet.)*

BETTY. Carl —

CARL. She deserves it.

BETTY. All right. I — I'll bring out the tray. It'll look more natural — a woman bringing out a tray.

CARL. Yes. We'll — we'll do this just this once. Then we'll have a lovely home. *(Betty nods. Carl goes into the yard. To Paul.)* Betty's coming with the drinks. Everything's under control. *(Carl goes and turns on the Malibu lights. The sun is starting to get red in the sky. In the kitchen, Betty takes two more pellets from the box of poison. She drops one into a glass.)*

BETTY. To Carl, from Carl's little pussy. *(She drops a second pellet into the wine bottle.)* And don't forget Sister's little pussies. *(Betty picks up the tray with four glasses and the wine bottle, then goes out into the yard. Sister comes down the outside staircase wearing a tinsel wig. She looks shaken and shattered.)*

CARL. Ah, the wine.

PAUL. How nice. *(Betty sets down the tray and very carefully starts handing out glasses of wine.)*

CARL. It's blue wine from the Napa Valley. You can drink it and not get drunk.

PAUL. Does it have alcohol?

CARL. Two hundred proof.

PAUL. Why don't you get drunk?

CARL. It's a metabolic wonder.

38

BETTY. Cheers, everyone!

CARL. To Furniture World! *(Everyone clinks glasses.)*

ALL. Cheers./ Cheers./ Cheers./ Cheers./ *(A beat. Sister, Betty and Carl drink their wine. Paul fakes a stumble and his wine goes flying.)*

PAUL. Oops! Gosh! Lost my balance. 'Least I saved the glass. *(A difficult pause.)*
Now when shall we have the wedding?

SISTER. You still want the wedding?

PAUL. What? Of course I do. Don't toy with me. Here, let's have a toast to our eternal union. *(Paul pours everyone more wine.)*

CARL. Ah, yes! To the wedding couple.

BETTY. To love throughout the ages.

CARL. To people who need people.

BETTY. Cheers! *(They all toast. Carl, Sister and Paul drink their drinks. Betty brings hers to her lips then stops.)* I think, if no one minds, I'll feed my wine to Sister's darling little kitties. After all, they should be a part of the celebration. *(Betty gives her wine to the cats in the cage. Paul looks at her suspiciously.)*

PAUL. Betty —

BETTY. What? Yes? *(Carl and Sister begin to groan and reel around the yard.)*

SISTER. I don't feel so good.

CARL. Oh my goodness. Whoa, my gut. I feel kinda like I've been poisoned. Betty?

PAUL. *(Starting to feel strange.)* You did something …

BETTY. Sister, you'd better check on your cats. They don't look so good.

SISTER. My cats? My cats — Garfield and Plums. *(Sister runs to the cat cage.)* Oh no. Oh no.

PAUL. *(Getting sicker by the minute.)* You double-crossing bitch. What's wrong with you?

BETTY. I guess I lost my balance. Oops.

SISTER. My cats are dead! *(Sister holds up two fat, furry, horrible looking, fake dead cats. Carl staggers over to Betty and shoves her to the ground.)*

CARL. I trusted you.

PAUL. *(Producing a gun.)* Does anybody mind if I shoot her?

CARL. Be my guest.

BETTY. No — *(Paul shoots Betty several times, emptying his gun into various portions of her body. She dies lavishly.)* Aah! Shit. Oh shit.

CARL. Shut up. You deserve it. *(Carl goes into the kitchen and starts pouring the contents of various strange bottles into a big pot on the stove. Betty lies bleeding to death in the yard. Sister is cramped with pain.)*

SISTER. You shot her.

PAUL. Sure. She killed your cats. I won't allow anyone to ever kill your cats again.

SISTER. You won't?

PAUL. *(As he falls to the ground.)* No. I'll take special good care of you as long as I live. For the rest of my life; until I'm dead and gone; till my very last breath is drawn.

SISTER. Then you forgive me?

PAUL. Oh yes.

SISTER. I'm innocent.

PAUL. Completely.

SISTER. And we're in love?

PAUL. Yes, love, yes.

SISTER. Then I don't care that we're dying. I don't care. It's like living to me. It's like being born fresh from the ground. *(In the kitchen, Carl has prepared an antidote to the poison. He drinks a healthy dose of the potion and is quickly revived.)*

CARL. Ahh, yes! *(He brings the pot outside, stirring it with a strange object.)* Sister — *(Sister pulls herself to her feet.)*

SISTER. Carl, I'm innocent. All is forgiven. Finally, he loves me and all is forgiven. Let's celebrate! Let's celebrate! *(Sister lurches up the outside staircase, alternately dancing and cramping in pain. Carl looks at Paul.)*

CARL. *(To Paul.)* I have the antidote.

PAUL. For the poison?

CARL. But you have to pay. *(Sister reels to her window. She throws out handfuls of red glitter. She is laughing and coughing and gasping for air, as she watches the glitter fall.)*

SISTER. Innocence is proclaimed! The verdict is not guilty! And someone could love me after all. After all …

CARL. Hey! Hey, Sister. You're wrong. You're very wrong.

SISTER. No, no, a thousand times …

CARL. He doesn't love you. He's nothing more than an opportunist. He's just using you to get your money. Your inheritance.

SISTER. *(Overlapping.)* No, please, don't let me know. Just keep it a secret. I can die very soon.

CARL. Tell her, Paul.

PAUL. What?

CARL. How you feel about her. Exactly how you feel about her.

SISTER. Please, let it be a secret. A secret. I'll be good. Sshh! Sshh!

PAUL. I don't love you. You're pathetic. I just wanted your money. I was using you the whole time. You're nothing to me. Nothing to me but unfinished toast.

CARL. *(To Sister.)* I think it was time you heard the truth.

PAUL. *(About the antidote.)* I need that now.

CARL. I know you do, Paul. But I want you to crawl for it. Can you do that? Can you crawl for it? Let's see your crawl. Get down on your knees. Now crawl. *(Carl extends a lifelike rubber vibrator out to Paul. Paul starts crawling to Carl. As Carl stirs the potion with the vibrator.)* Watch this, Sister. Watch this puppy crawl.

SISTER. I knew it all along. I saw them kissing in the garden. They were kissing in the garden. Sucking fruits. Suck, suck, slurp, slurp. *(Paul has crawled up to Carl. Carl takes the vibrator out of the pot and lets Paul suck the potion off the rubber cock. Sister falls and lurches down the stairway as she delivers the rest of her speech.)* Mashing fruits in each other's faces, red with juices, swollen with heavy bruises. Why do I forget I've forgotten what I see? All along; all along I don't remember I forgot ...

CARL. *(To Paul.)* Good dog. He's a good dog. *(Carl takes the vibrator out of Paul's mouth and kicks Paul to the ground.)* Sister, what do you think? Should I kill him or let him go?

SISTER. *(Weakly.)* ... Whatever you think.

CARL. *(To Paul.)* Get outta here. You deserve to live. *(Paul leaves the yard in a sick sweat. Sister lies dying at the foot of the outdoor stairway. Carl takes the pot over to her. He scoops up handfuls of the potion for her to drink.)* There, there. I'll take care of you, Little Scampy. Just like I always have. I'm the only one who ever looked out for you. I'm the only one who ever will. There. Is that better now? Are you better?

SISTER. Yes. I — better.

CARL. Good. Then could you go make me a shake? I need my shake.

SISTER. Yeah. Sure, sure. I know you like your shake. *(She gets up and starts for the kitchen.)*

CARL. Wait. Before you go, I want you to put on those underpants.

SISTER. They're still wet.

CARL. Put them on anyway. It's not decent for you to go around without anything on underneath. It could get you in big trouble. *(Sister puts on the wet underpants.)* Ha, ha, ha, ha!

SISTER. What?

CARL. Nothing. I just liked seeing that slime crawl to me. It was nice. I had him under control. *(Sister goes into the kitchen to make Carl his shake.)*

SISTER. *(Spaghetti/Pinkie.)* [P] I'm thinking I'm remembering forgetting./ [SP] Ssh. Bury the hatchet./ [P] I did. I buried it. It's breathing though. It's buried and breathing./ [SP] Ssh. Don't speak. Speaking is evil./ [P] I know nothing to speak of, but this I can say — there are scars on my tonsils from secret screaming./ [SP] Sssh. *(Sister turns on the shake machine. Rumbling sounds, as though the earth was breaking open; tinkling glass about to shatter, cracking wood; a faraway shriek. Sister turns off the machine. She pours the shake into a glass. She puts several pellets of poison into the glass, then picks up a giant butcher knife and walks outside carrying the shake and concealing the knife.)* Here's your shake.

CARL. Thanks, Little Rascal. *(Carl drinks his shake.)*

SISTER. Carl, I wanna ask you something. And I need you to speak the truth.

CARL. You can always believe me.

SISTER. But what if what you say isn't true?

CARL. That's when you have to take the leap of faith. That's something they teach you in church. *(Sister brings out the knife and gingerly threatens him with it.)*

SISTER. You hurt me, didn't you?

CARL. No. When?

SISTER. I don't know when, but you did it.

CARL. *(About the knife.)* Put that down.

SISTER. I don't think so.

CARL. *(His stomach starts to cramp.)* Ooh.

42

SISTER. What's the matter? Tummyache?

CARL. Yes — I — Did you ... ? I need the — *(Carl reaches for the pot containing the antidote. Sister kicks the pot over. The potion spills out across the yard.)*

SISTER. Get away from that!

CARL. Hey! Look. What do you want?

SISTER. Tell me about it.

CARL. What?

SISTER. When you hurt me. When I was little. *(Threatening him with the knife.)* Tell me.

CARL. I — I guess. Once I ...

SISTER. What? I want to know.

CARL. It was when you were sleeping.

SISTER. I was sleeping?

CARL. Yes, I — I sodomized you once when you were sleeping.

SISTER. I didn't wake up? That seems like something if someone were doing it to you — you would wake up.

CARL. I was very gentle. I went slow. You slept like a baby.

SISTER. I didn't stir?

CARL. You didn't stir.

SISTER. And that was the only time.

CARL. Virtually.

SISTER. What do you mean?

CARL. Occasionally, I'd come in your room in the morning and I'd let you suck me. You'd swallow every drop like feeding milk to a hungry baby.

SISTER. But I must have — was I asleep?

CARL. You were drowsy.

SISTER. Drowsy. I was drowsy. And that was all?

CARL. Virtually. Except for when I'd pick you up from school and take you out in my pickup truck and fuck you good.

SISTER. But every day you came for me. Every day you picked me up from school.

CARL. Virtually.

SISTER. And even still.

CARL. Yes, still, yes.

SISTER. This is very bad.

CARL. Yes. *(Sister waves the knife across her body.)*

SISTER. I've been touched by evil. All over. Every place.

CARL. Forgive me. I wanted to show you the ropes. I thought that's what I was doing — showing you the ropes.

SISTER. I hate you! I hate you! I need to kill you!

CARL. Please, don't. Forgive me. Please, forgive me. *(Sister stalks Carl. He lurches away from her and trips and falls into his own shit.)* Oh, God! God! Shit! Don't kill me! Please, Sister, I'll do anything! Don't kill me!

SISTER. I have to kill you. I have to. Because I have to kill you! *(Carl tries to get away from her. He throws himself into the bushes. She lunges in the bushes after him and stabs him over and over and over again.)*

CARL.	SISTER.
No! No! Forgive me!	You're a bad egg, a rotten
Help me. Forgive me!	apple in a barrel!
	I'm sorry to say this man was
	less than dirt and we had
	to put him away for good.

SISTER. *(Pinkie/Spaghetti.)* [P] I didn't mean it./ [SP] Yes, you did./ [P] Help me./ [SP] We have to leave. *(Sister takes off her dress and shoes.)* We're leaving this garden of sorrow. This dump yard of despair./ [P] How will we go?/ [SP] We'll fly./ [P] My wings aren't ready yet. They're on order, but they haven't arrived./ [SP] We'll go without wings. We've done it before./ [P] When?/ *(A flying harness is lowered from the grid. Sister climbs into the flying contraption.)* [SP] There was a time once long ago and pain was like glass stuck inside, but it didn't hurt — no hurt — because we were not home. We were flying./ [P] Yes. I remember. Yes. Dash away, dash away. That's what they tell to the reindeer. A whisper to the deer. Remember the story? It was in the story. The pages of old. Dash away./ [SP] Yes./ *(She flies out over the audience.)* [P] Oh, we're flying! Look, we're off towards home. And I can grasp stars with my hands and shells with my toes — pink shells; angel kisses. *(She suddenly stops flying as she spots the deserted dress below.)* Oh no. Oh, wait. There's someone, she's down there. Who's down there?/ [SP] It's Sister. You remember Sister./ [P] A long time ago there was a Sister./ [SP] And now she knows./ [P] Knows what?/ [SP] Everything./ [P] I remember everything. We must go back for her./ [SP] We can't. We're escaping. Now fly! Please, fly!/ [P] But she's down there! She's down there!/ [SP] We'll die. It will kill us. Oh. Oh. Oh. Oh./ [P] Oh. No. Please come! *(She flies down, grabs the dress, then sweeps back up, sailing with the dress in her arms.)* I remember you. I remember you. You had short yellow hair and you pressed flowers with rocks and you dreamed one day you would become an astronaut, but things were bad and for a long time you were afraid. I remember you. Very well. I remember you. *(She dances across the firmament with her dress. Lights fade to blackout.)*

End of Play

PROPERTY LIST

Toy china tea set for 2 (BETTY)
Dinner bell (BETTY)
Plate of ginger snaps (BETTY)
Sampler in frame (BETTY)
Plastic briefcase (CARL)
Milk shake machine, drinking glass, milk shake (BETTY)
Brochures (CARL)
Shovel, excrement, garbagement (SISTER)
Big soggy sponge (CARL)
Bowl of red M&Ms (SISTER)
Underpants (SISTER)
Wigs (SISTER)
Bubble liquid, frying pan (BETTY)
Basket (BETTY)
Carrots (SISTER)
2 fat cats, cage (SISTER)
Grocery bag, cans of string beans (BETTY)
Can of poison pellets (CARL, BETTY, SISTER)
Sack (CARL)
Bra, petticoat, high heels, dangling earrings, pink evening dress
    (SISTER)
Giant engagement ring (PAUL)
Frilly apron, plate of canapes (BETTY)
Legal papers (PAUL)
Pens (BETTY, CARL)
Cookie tray, burnt gingerbread men (SISTER)
Tray and 4 glasses (CARL, BETTY)
Blue wine (CARL)
3 burning cigarettes, drawer of cigarette butts (SISTER)
Malibu lights (CARL)
Gun (PAUL)
Strange bottles of liquid, a pot (CARL)
Red glitter (SISTER)
Rubber vibrating dildo (CARL)
Giant butcher knife (SISTER)
Flying harness (SISTER)

SOUND EFFECTS

Shake machine
Deranged laughter, violent sex, roller-coaster sounds
Birds chirping at sunrise
Cats shrieking
Tinkling glass, cracking wood, shriek

L-PLAY

L-PLAY was originally produced by the Berkshire Theatre Festival (Arthur Storch, Artistic Director: Kate Maguire, Managing Director) in Stockbridge, Massachusetts, in 1995. It was directed by Eric Hill; the set design was by Gary M. English; the lighting design was by Phil Monat; the costume design was by Pamela Scofield; the sound design was by James Wildman. The cast was as follows:

Actress A	Allyn Rose
Actress B	Jennifer Thomas
Actress C	Nicole Bradin
Actor A	John Lenartz
Actor B	Duane Noch
Actor C	Jonathan Uffelman

CHARACTERS

The play requires three actresses and three actors:

Actress A plays MONICA, LUNATIC.
Actress B plays JOAN, GRANDDAUGHTER, SMALL ONE, LUCHEEA.
Actress C plays GERTRUDE, GRANDMOTHER, SHELLY, MIDDLE ONE.

Actor A plays PRICE, MALCOLM, BEN, BIG ONE.
Actor B plays JAY, WES, SHOE.
Actor C plays VARIOUS PARTS, LEARNER, NARRATOR.

Scene 1: Loneliness — MONICA, JOAN, PRICE

Scene 2: Linked — JAY, GERTRUDE

Scene 3: Loser — MALCOLM, VARIOUS PARTS

Scene 4: Lunatic, Part One — LUNATIC

Scene 5: Learner, Part One — LEARNER

Scene 6: Lost — BEN, WESLEY, SHELLY

Scene 7: Lunatic, Part Two — LUNATIC

Scene 8: Leaving — GRANDMOTHER, GRANDDAUGHTER

Scene 9: Learner, Part Two — LEARNER

Scene 10: Life — NARRATOR, BIG ONE, MIDDLE ONE, SMALL ONE

Scene 11: Lunatic, Part Three — LUNATIC

Scene 12: Learner, Part Three — LEARNER, LUCHEEA

AUTHOR'S NOTE: The idea of this piece is that each scene is brought vividly and singularly to life through lights, costumes, sound, style and tone. However, the fragmented nature of the play necessitates production elements be selective and sparse, so that the play keeps moving.

L-PLAY

Scene 1

LONELINESS

Sounds: winter winds, distant train, dogs barking, church bells clanging. Time: Christmas Eve, the past. Place: Pitt's Diner, South Louisiana. Lights up slowly on Monica Fench, thirties, an attractive but worn-out woman wearing a faded waitress uniform and talking into a black phone.

MONICA. *(Into phone.)* 'Cause Mama doesn't want me. She doesn't want me. No, because remember last year? … Well, did she say she wanted me? … Uh-huh, well then, she doesn't want me. Anyway, Lou Ellen, it doesn't matter 'cause I can't 'cause I'm working. I got to stay here and serve people … Sure. Three old ladies just left. They left me a fifteen cent tip. I swear I'm holding three nickels right here. *(She gestures with an empty hand.)*
 … No, baby. Mr. Pitt's not here. He had to spend Christmas Eve with his wife, ex-wife, and kids … I didn't wanna go. Their house smells like lavender piss … No, everything's real wonderful. I'm expecting Mr. Pitt's gonna give me a ring for Christmas … Of course you'll be invited to our wedding, you're my own sweet child … I don't know about afterward. Maybe you could visit us some … I said maybe; look, Lou Ellen, I got some people here … She does? All right … Merry Christmas, Mama, how're you? … Well, of course I'm gonna send Lou Ellen something for Christmas. I looked. I'm still looking. I just can't seem to pick out what's right … No, I've got a job. Still working at Mr. Pitt's Diner … Well, it's better than scraping shit at Parchment Penitentiary … What you don't understand is I've already made something out of my life.

I've been somebody and done some things and that's just what I'm trying to recover from … Uh-huh, I know that's how you think … You're gonna tell Lou Ellen what? You'll tell her the wool muffler's from me? Well, thanks, Mama. What color is it? Just so I'll know … Okay. 'Bye. *(She hangs up.)* Yellow's not her color. She'll never wear it. *(Joan Wells, fourteen, enters the diner. She is bundled up in second-hand winter wear. Her face is flushed from the cold.)*

JOAN. Merry Christmas.

MONICA. Have a seat. There's a Christmas Eve special.

JOAN. I don't have any money.

MONICA. Well, none of the stuff is free.

JOAN. That would be funny. I mean, if it was.

MONICA. Well, then I guess it ain't funny.

JOAN. No, I know it ain't. I come t'see William Pitt.

MONICA. He's not here.

JOAN. 'Cause I'm his granddaughter, Joan Wells. I'm arranged to come stay with him after the New Year, but I come on early so as not to miss Christmas.

MONICA. I've heard about you. You've been in trouble.

JOAN. Not much. Some.

MONICA. He had to sign some paper to keep you out of some big trouble.

JOAN. I come on early because of Christmas I guess is what happened.

MONICA. He's not even sure you're his granddaughter. He never married that woman.

JOAN. I know.

MONICA. So you're a bastard.

JOAN. No, ma'am, my mama was a bastard. Me, I just don't have any family. Except for this one grandpaw.

MONICA. His name's Mr. Pitt.

JOAN. Mr. Pitt. He used to visit them I know. One time he took them to the state fair and no one could guess his age.

MONICA. I don't know how happy he's gonna be about you coming here. Before you were expected. Where're your things?

JOAN. I left them behind.

MONICA. Are you on the lam?

JOAN. No, ma'am.

MONICA. I don't like this.

JOAN. It's how it is, I guess. *(Price Summers, thirties, enters. He is dressed for the cold weather. There is something unsettling and inappropriate about his genial exuberance.)*

PRICE. I come for the Christmas Eve special.

MONICA. All right.

PRICE. Do I know you?

MONICA. Uh-huh.

PRICE. *(To Joan.)* Do I know you?

JOAN. Maybe. I don't know.

PRICE. Well, something seems familiar.

MONICA. What would you like to drink?

PRICE. Milk.

MONICA. Small, medium, or large?

PRICE. Large, I believe, let's have a large. No. A small. *(Monica exits.)*

JOAN. *(To Price.)* Would you like me to pray for you? Every day three times a day all through next year for just one dollar?

PRICE. What would you pray for?

JOAN. Whatever you like, mister. You name the bill. I'll fill it.

PRICE. I don't believe in church.

JOAN. Prayers ain't church.

PRICE. How 'bout fifty cents? How much would that get me?

JOAN. Same. I'd pray for you the same.

PRICE. Do it then. *(He tosses her a fifty-cent piece. Monica enters with a small glass of milk.)*

MONICA. Here's your milk.

JOAN. I'd like one too, miss.

MONICA. Cost money.

JOAN. *(Showing her the coin.)* Here. *(Monica exits to the kitchen.)*

PRICE. Those curls don't flatter her. She used to be an attractive woman. She doesn't remember me. We worked together on Senator Emiling's campaign. He was a great man, Senator Emiling. He knew everything about life. All of its ins and outs. Most people aren't versed in the important things, but he was. He knew. He could make things stick.

JOAN. That's good.

PRICE. A whole crowd of us would put in hours of volunteer labor. Mailing out flyers, handing out buttons, nailing posters up on telephone poles. I had twenty-seven bumper stickers on my car. It was a united front. We'd work late and have to order in sandwiches from a restaurant. Monica was one of the ringleaders. She was awfully pretty back then. *(Monica enters with a medium glass of milk.)*

MONICA. *(To Joan.)* I brought you a medium.

JOAN. Thank you, ma'am.

PRICE. Monica. You don't remember me. We worked on Senator Emiling's campaign together. You'd always want a tuna fish sandwich, that was your favorite. And an ice tea. Lots of sugar.

MONICA. You want white meat; dark meat? You can get mixed on the special.

PRICE. Get it mixed?

MONICA. Yeah.

PRICE. The Senator hung himself over her. She turned him in to get leniency and he hung himself with a necktie.

MONICA. You got that wrong.

PRICE. Did it with the necktie she gave him.

MONICA. Had nothing to do with me.

PRICE. He was a great man. Had plans for change. He saw hope and goodness where others did not.

MONICA. Hey, I don't wanna serve you. Now why don't you go? *(Price threatens her with a gun.)*

PRICE. I've been waiting to kill you for what you did to him. It tore everything apart. Say you're sorry.

MONICA. I'm sorry.

PRICE. Do you mean it?

MONICA. Yes, I'm sorry.

PRICE. You have to tell people what they want to hear or they don't come back. *(He shoots her.)* I had to do it. I had to do it. See if she's dead. *(Joan goes over to the body.)*

JOAN. She's dead.

PRICE. Shake her. Make sure. Shake her. *(Joan shakes the body.)*

JOAN. Uh-huh, she is.

PRICE. You. You're a bad luck penny.

JOAN. I know.

PRICE. Pray for me. You owe it.

JOAN. Heavenly Father, accept our thanks for this food and all our many other blessings. In Jesus' name, we pray. For Thou art the kingdom, and the power, and the glory ... *(Price exits. Joan kneels beside Monica's body.)* Don't worry. I'm not gonna pray for him. Far as I'm concerned, he's wasted his money.

Scene 2

LINKED

Sounds — back alley noises: vague flamenco music; cat screeching; traffic; infant crying; a neighbor's hacking cough. Time: Late night. Place: L.A., a cheap apartment. Gertrude, thirties, paces around the apartment perspiring from the heat. She wears cut-off shorts and a T-shirt. Her sweat-drenched hair knotted on top of her head. Jay, thirties, sits at a table scribbling on a torn grocery bag. Both of them have been drinking sherry.

JAY. *(Writing maniacally.)* One moment, okay? One moment ... Okay, continue.
GERTRUDE. *(Listening to the awful coughing emanating from the alley.)* It's impossible. Do you believe that? She's literally dying of smoker's consumption — hacker's cough.
JAY. Shut the window.
GERTRUDE. I can't, it's over a hundred degrees or something.
JAY. It doesn't affect me. I must be numb. Continue, please.
GERTRUDE. *(Yelling out the window.)* I wish you would die! Why don't you cough yourself into a coma and die!? *(The coughing subsides.)* Oh, if only I could breathe or think or know anything, where were we?
JAY. *(Reading.)* "Even though I care for you, I have to admit you're unseasoned."
GERTRUDE. Oh, right. *(Dictating.)* Even though I care for you, I have to admit you're unseasoned ... *(A beat.)* In a few years, perhaps after some hours on the couch, you may possibly evolve into

a semblance of a human being. *(A beat.)* In the meantime, I must seek a spiritually and sexually fulfilling relationship elsewhere among the living. *(Beat.)* Sincerely yours, Jay S.

JAY. *(Writing quickly.)* All right, good. Good. Good. This is good, I think. I'll have to recopy. Bloodstains. I mean because she didn't even give me time … All my things … The things I left. I didn't see it coming, but it was, you see, in retrospect I remember things. And she kept suggesting to me, for my New Year's resolution, she kept suggesting I should try to become a more authentic person.

GERTRUDE. Well, you are authentic.

JAY. I think so. But women, they can make you doubt the nose on your face. I mean I actually went around for several days trying to be more authentic, but I'm sorry, I'm sorry, I didn't know how.

GERTRUDE. It's a blessing she threw you out. It's hard to see now, but in the long run you'll understand this is your lucky day.

JAY. I know you're right. I just can't see it. She had such a great body.

GERTRUDE. But she wouldn't fuck you.

JAY. Right.

GERTRUDE. She withheld sex. You had to beg; you had to plead. And still she said, "No." Now do you want me to tell you something awful that will make you feel a whole lot better?

JAY. Yes.

GERTRUDE. She's going to be fired.

JAY. Really?

GERTRUDE. The Research Center is making major cutbacks and it's no secret she's got serious attitude problems.

JAY. Katrina's being fired?

GERTRUDE. Next week.

JAY. Who will make my car payments?

GERTRUDE. I'll help.

JAY. If it wasn't for you, Gertrude, I'd think women were all bags of remorseless shit.

GERTRUDE. And yet I'm so lonely.

JAY. Didn't you go out with Alan? How did that go? *(Gertrude reacts with mad abandon: retching and gagging and pulling at her hair.)* What? What? He's not so bad. He lent me money and one of his ties …

GERTRUDE. Oh, stop, stop! Please! I have to beg you. Because

58

I would never ... Alan! Really! Didn't I tell you? We were out —
this is so horrible — at this restaurant and he couldn't get over it
because I had ordered a BLT with fries and he had ordered a
Spanish omelette and hash browns and, oh my, he went on and on
just on and on about how he wished he'd ordered the BLT and the
Spanish omelette was made with canned tomatoes and couldn't he
have just one of my fries because the hash browns weren't even
crisp, until I thought I would ... No, really, shoot me if I ever ...
I mean he ate half the plate of fries which were practically unsal-
vageable because he had salted with such ferocity ...

JAY. He salted your French fries?

GERTRUDE. That's the kind of person ...

JAY. Well, no, you're right.

GERTRUDE. And we are not talking moderate salting. I mean
this was ... *(She mimes reckless dumping of salt.)*

JAY. Yes, I know. But still I think, I think still, your standards are
too high.

GERTRUDE. Too high? How can they be too high? I was with
you, wasn't I?

JAY. Yes, but I wasn't so bad back then.

GERTRUDE. You were worse. Please. No, please. Here, let's
make a list. Let's make a list of men I should date. Men who are
worthy of me.

JAY. All right.

GERTRUDE. How about ... how about Jasper Johns? I love how
he finds the divine in the ordinary.

JAY. I think he's dead and he's gay. But I'll put him down.

GERTRUDE. How about Ad Reinhardt? I love all those black
paintings. The variations, the depth ...

JAY. Dead.

GERTRUDE. Well, you think of someone.

JAY. Sugar Ray Leonard.

GERTRUDE. Hmm. Maybe. Is he married?

JAY. We could check. At least he's alive.

GERTRUDE. This is depressing. "Only connect." "Only connect."
Who said...?

JAY. E.M. Forster.

GERTRUDE. Dead.

JAY. Very.

GERTRUDE. Right.

JAY. But you shouldn't give up.

GERTRUDE. No I won't. I'm a Capricorn. They don't give up. I hate it when people give up; after that there's so little left to do.

JAY. God, do you think Butch and I still have a chance?

GERTRUDE. Butch?

JAY. That's what I call Katrina. Sometimes I call her Butch.

GERTRUDE. Really?

JAY. Yeah.

GERTRUDE. I thought you didn't like nicknames. You said nicknames demean a person's dignity. They infantilize relationships. Turn people into pets.

JAY. I said that?

GERTRUDE. Yes. Remember, you wouldn't let me call you Ding.

JAY. I didn't like you calling me that. It always sounded obscene. It made me want to cover your mouth and go Ssh! Ssh! Ssh!

GERTRUDE. Butch! I mean what did you say? What did you say? That she didn't know the difference between ephemeral and diaphanous. Or she mistook opaque for translucent?! God! If you think about it, I mean just don't think about it too hard or you might regret. Big, big, big! Regret! Remember when you told me I reminded you of my dog?

JAY. How much have you been drinking?

GERTRUDE. I don't know.

JAY. Oh.

GERTRUDE. Why do you ask?

JAY. It's just your family are all alcoholics. You have the genes. You're susceptible, I believe. Wasn't your mother a drunk?

GERTRUDE. She always liked you. She said you reminded her of an old Dutch uncle, how you'd sit in the corner and ignore everyone.

JAY. Remember when you fell down all those stairs at the Ahmanson and I had to wash off your knees in the pond …

GERTRUDE. Fountain.

JAY. That was a warning sign. You should have taken heed.

GERTRUDE. You are really making me want to drink very badly. But look at this! You've hogged the sherry. It was mine. A gift from a dear friend. Brought back to me from Spain. Spanish sherry. You can't even get it here.

JAY. Who do you know that went to Spain?

GERTRUDE. I met someone who went to Spain.

JAY. Oh.

GERTRUDE. Nothing serious ... a fleeting speck.

JAY. It doesn't ... Believe me, it doesn't ... I mean there is no residue.

GERTRUDE. I know. Oh, I know. That's why we're such good friends. But I do want to save the bottle. Put a candle in it. Let it drip. Different colors. Let them drip.

JAY. I've seen bottles like that. I used to have one.

GERTRUDE. Yeah.

JAY. Nice those.

GERTRUDE. Yeah. *(Loud sounds of an old woman's horrendous hacking cough.)* God, she's still alive. Isn't it awful?!

JAY. Yes.

GERTRUDE. God, it's awful.

JAY. Yes, yes, yes, it is.

Scene 3

LOSER

In the following scene, all of the parts except Malcolm are played by the same actor. The actor wears dark, neutral cloth-ing and distinguishes each character by the use of a large, white handkerchief. Malcolm, the loser, wears an overcoat and funny shoes. Time: Later than you think. Place: Street, Chatwick's home, the street. Sounds: Street noises, including horse hooves hitting pavement, horns beeping, traffic, ven-dors. Fractured light scatters, swirls across the stage. Malcolm comes to center stage. A pinlight illuminates his face.

MALCOLM. Shoe Boy! Shoe Boy! Shoe polish! *(Shoe boy appears. He begins to polish Malcolm's shoes with a white rag.)*
SHOE BOY. Today's your party day.
MALCOLM. Yes, I have an invitation. Mr. Chatwick has invited me. It's an intimate affair. From what I understand, Mr. Umpton was not included.
SHOE BOY. *(Completing his job.)* Good as new.
MALCOLM. Thank you, Shoe Boy. *(Shoe Boy exits.)* Now what can I do to make this a wonderful day? *(Mrs. Pepper appears wearing a white kerchief around her head.)*
MRS. PEPPER. Hello, Malcolm!
MALCOLM. Mrs. Pepper! How are you?
MRS. PEPPER. Back in my own backyard, eating peppers from my pepper tree.
MALCOLM. Everyone to his own taste! *(Then, to himself.)* Or whatever one says to get down the road. *(Back to Mrs. Pepper.)* I'm off to a party at Mr. Chatwick's. I'll have some news for you when I return. *(Mrs. Pepper exits.)* Imagine this, my heart is beating. Strange the reactions we have when we're about to have a wonderful experience. *(He knocks. Loud sound of knocking. A beat.)* Perhaps they didn't hear. No, I knocked loudly. Sufficiently loud, I believe. *(A beat.)* Perhaps not. *(He knocks again. Deafening sound of knocking.)* I hope I didn't overdo it. I don't want to appear anxious. Wouldn't look good. I hope I've come at the proper time. Perhaps it was another day. It's possible to make such errors. Such idiotic blunders. *(Frantically, he searches for his invitation. He produces it and reads it over carefully.)* No. Here. I'm correct; I should be here; I'm expected. My invitation. My invitation. What's this? A bell. A bell, of course. *(He rings. Unspeakably loud clanging of bells.)* I'm overheated. These shoes say too much. They're not subtle. I'll change. But is there time? They might be coming to the door. What do you expect? You just rang the bell! Please, stand here, please stand here, stand here, please, and don't think about your feet. *(A butler appears with a white napkin draped over his arm.)*
BUTLER. Good day. Won't you come in?
MALCOLM. Thank you.
BUTLER. Shall I take your coat?
MALCOLM. Not at the moment. You see, I have some things in

my pockets.

BUTLER. Would you like a drink?

MALCOLM. Whiskey.

BUTLER. Certainly.

MALCOLM. Oh, Butler. Where are the other guests?

BUTLER. Milling in the parlor.

MALCOLM. Has Umpton arrived?

BUTLER. Mr. Umpton has not been invited. *(Butler exits.)*

MALCOLM. Not been invited, I see. Whereas, I am here. Perhaps my clothes are somewhat shabby underneath this coat. And my shoes are vivid, ostentatious, even vulgar. Yet I am invited. I'm included in the gathering. *(A Woman appears waving a white handkerchief.)*

WOMAN. Have you been in the gallery?

MALCOLM. No.

WOMAN. Imagine Chatwick inviting us all over here to try and sell us his terrible little paintings in those vilely expensive frames. Crass is the word. And the subject matter!

MALCOLM. I haven't seen.

WOMAN. Ditches. Green ditches, brown ditches, yellow ditches. Variation: tree trunks crossing bigger, greener, browner ditches. Chatwick is such an ass. Don't you agree?

MALCOLM. Off the record, of course.

WOMAN. Oh, you are clever. Have we met?

MALCOLM. No.

WOMAN. Good. I'm going to walk right out this door and wait for you in the rose garden. I'll be waiting for you completely naked; so don't be long. I'll be standing among the damask variety. *(She exits.)*

MALCOLM. I knew it would be like this when I made it to the top. Just as I planned. Only better. *(Butler enters.)*

BUTLER. Your whiskey, sir.

MALCOLM. Thank you.

BUTLER. Mr. Chatwick will now see you in his study. This way, please. *(They proceed to spiral endlessly around the stage.)* Ha, ha, ha, ha!

MALCOLM. What?

BUTLER. Pardon me, sir, I was remembering a funny I heard in the cook's quarters.

MALCOLM. Keep it to yourself.

BUTLER. Apologies, sir.

MALCOLM. Umph.

BUTLER. We have arrived. Mr. Chatwick will be with you in a moment. *(Butler exits.)*

MALCOLM. I have arrived. The inner sanctum. I have arrived. A view. Look. A view. The water. The mountains. Sky. Standing here with my whiskey among comfortable furniture; admiring the view. *(Chatwick enters wearing a white bow tie. A crisp white handkerchief sticks out of his breast pocket.)*

CHATWICK. Malcolm, very good.

MALCOLM. Mr. Chatwick. So kind of you to invite me.

CHATWICK. Of course. Now may I tell you something? A piece of information that will serve you for as long as you live.

MALCOLM. Oh yes. Please do, sir. Please do.

CHATWICK. You must always tell people what they want to hear or they don't come back.

MALCOLM. Very good. Very wise.

CHATWICK. A practical fact.

MALCOLM. It shall be my motto.

CHATWICK. A shame you didn't learn it sooner. Possibly I would have been able to renew your contract.

MALCOLM. My contract? You're not renewing my contract.

CHATWICK. No.

MALCOLM. I'm slightly confused. Then I — I'm getting a new contract with the promotion?

CHATWICK. Umpton's getting the promotion. He doesn't want you on his team.

MALCOLM. Then I ... I ...

CHATWICK. Yes, you shall be fired.

MALCOLM. But Mr. Chatwick, I beg you, please, reconsider, please. I've worked for you for seventeen years. I'm devoted to your firm. I love our organization. Every day I am happy to go there and work my hardest. I promise I've learned my lesson. From now on, I shall always only tell people what they want to hear. If I have a doubt as to what that is, I shall ask them specifically and make certain. It was — I know — the Stillers. I told them what

64

the costs were actually going to be; I should have — I know this now — I should have told them the costs were what they wanted them to be. Yes! Very careless of me. Wrong, wrong! Shame! Shame! Go to the back of the class!

CHATWICK. Calm down now, Malcolm. Calm down. Rest assured, the Stillers are reasonable people. The objection there was a shaved pimple on your neck.

MALCOLM. Where?

CHATWICK. It's gone now. It's healed. But there was one. We saw it.

MALCOLM. Yes, well, I see.

CHATWICK. Very good then. It's settled. Let's go down and join the party.

MALCOLM. I believe I'll decline.

CHATWICK. But I've invited you. You're expected.

MALCOLM. I ... Excuse me, sir, but wasn't I just asked here to be fired?

CHATWICK. Malcolm, you do amuse me. Would I invite you here just to fire you? Heavens, no! Why, I've bet on you!

MALCOLM. What? *(Sound of people partying.)* Everyone crowd around! Gather round! Here he is! The man who makes funny noises, disgusting noises! All emanating from his armpits!

MALCOLM. Mr. Chatwick, I hardly think ...

CHATWICK. Don't let me down now. I've bet on you. Yorkshire's bet me ten Z that such a feat is not possible. Ten thousand Z! Now go on, boy. But first you must remove your coat. *(Loud chants from the crowd. Malcolm removes his coat, revealing near nakedness covered by shabby rags. The crowd goes silent. Malcolm begins making flatulent sounds from underneath his armpits. At first, the noises are polite popping sounds. Slowly they grow into loud, cracking, giant sounds. The crowd roars with laughter and applause. Malcolm completely commits to playing the fool. The whole episode builds to a mad crescendo, then abruptly ceases. Malcolm picks up his coat and puts it on wearily. Mrs. Pepper appears.)*

MRS. PEPPER. Hello, Malcolm. How was the party?

MALCOLM. A colossal event.

MRS. PEPPER. Would you like a bucket of peppers from my pepper tree? Something to take home with you?

MALCOLM.   A bucket of peppers indeed! Pah! Pah! Pah! A bucket of peppers indeed. *(He stomps past her, furious with indignation.)*

Scene 4

LUNATIC, PART ONE

Sound: Daytime television talk shows. Flicker of blue screen TV light. The Lunatic appears holding a dirty mop. She is dressed as a frumpy housewife. Time: Now. Place: Suburbia.

LUNATIC.   At home, in my living room, I watched the brand-new mothers being interviewed on TV because bearing children had left them very, very fat. They had no self-esteem. It was a fact because of fat they didn't like themselves. And they weren't even happy with the young ones. They didn't say so, but I bet they wanted to smother them or something worse.

All of their husbands were skinny and had jobs where they worked. Up on the TV screen they showed pictures of the mothers before and after the nippers. Before they looked a lot thinner and much more fun-loving.

Most of the husbands I wouldn't want. A baby would be nice if it had personality and didn't make you fat. But they seem to, and then you might lose your self-esteem and have to look to your husband to be supportive.

Then it happened. I needed some products from the supermarket. I was buying a mop. It was poking out of my cart because of its length. I hadn't eaten all day. Actually, I'd had a fat-free muffin, but the point is I was light-headed and was driving the cart with some lack of caution and managed to swing the mop into the nose of a woman looking down at meat prices. She obviously had osteoporosis or some other fragile-bone disease because her nose crumbled right on the spot, and now it seems I'm culpable.

There were other, more chilling incidences. One morning I woke up with a start. I was in bed with a man or a woman. I couldn't guess who or where we were.

I was wearing roller skates and there was fruit all over the bed. Apple cores, oranges, pineapples, dates. I was shocked to see I had part of a banana up my "vagina," as they call it on the six o'clock news. Part of it seemed to have been eaten but this is, of course, conjecture. It was snowing outside, which was odd because the last thing I remembered was swatting flies in summer. *(Sound of flies swarming, swatting noises. Colored lights flicker. Blackout.)*

Scene 5

LEARNER, PART ONE

Lights up on the Learner, a pale, emaciated young man with glasses, sitting pensively onstage, thumbing through a slim volume of poetry. Time: Now. Place: College campus, Urbana.

LEARNER. I'm taking a class in Modern Poetry. Today I was happy to find "a poem can be anything." Apparently, a poem doesn't have to rhyme or even be words. It could be X's on a page. That would be a concrete poem. I thought it was more complex, more technical, something I wouldn't be able to grasp.

Another thing Professor Billings said, "T.S. Eliot is overrated." I considered that good news because I don't understand him anyway. There was this girl though ... the girl who wore the back brace. When she heard the recording of the "Proofrock" poem, soundless tears streamed down her face, her terribly red, blotchy face. But maybe it wasn't the poem. Maybe she'd had a romantic disappointment. Maybe she'd gotten bad news about the back situation. I wanted to, but I was afraid to speak to her. Afraid to eat the peach, or whatever.

I looked at her, then looked away. I started playing with a rubber band, twisting it around my fingers, snapping it ruthlessly.

Then she rose to leave the classroom, and I realized, I noticed, she was struggling with her books, her papers. Because of the back brace, balance was difficult to coordinate. I went to her rescue. Her name was Lucheea.

Every day I would meet Lucheea; I would help her with her books. Many books. Big, thick, heavy tomes, volumes. I suspected she wasn't reading them thoroughly. Perhaps she was checking them out to impress a certain other. But I don't know for certain. You never know for certain who has read a book. How much of it they have actually covered.

All the same, I loved her. Why should I care what she has or has not read with her brown eyes that won't look at me? Always protected by lids and lashes.

How I wanted to hold her pale face with my bony hands and stare into her eyes (brown her eyes!) until I would know her and she would see me too.

And then one day her back brace was removed. She was free to ambulate without obstruction. She claimed she no longer needed me to carry her books. She no longer wanted to walk slow and converse with me. I had to run after her. She could move very swift, even with all of those books. "What's that you're reading? Ah, Dostoyevsky. *The Idiot.* One of my favorites. The Volga. Gooseberries! Troika!"

Did she know I had never read it? Did she suspect that I have trouble reading the longer books? Holding them up with my frail wrists, reading the tiny print with my bad eyes. So many words I don't understand and I do not look up because dictionaries … well, just try to wrench one of those from a bedside table.

Lucheea, wait! I'm writing a poem! A poem inspired by you! Your name. Lucheea. The music of it. The music of you. Lucheea, Lucheea. My coy one! Lucheea! *(Lights quickly fade to black.)*

Scene 6

LOST

Sounds: Pool hall, pinball machine, beers sliding down a bar, country jukebox. Time: Summer. Place: Low-down bar. Two men — Ben, older, and Wes, younger — stand drinking local beer from bottles. A bar stool sits between them.

BEN. How do I know? How do I know? I looked.

WES. You looked?

BEN. Don't you ever look?

WES. It's usually dark.

BEN. Light a match. Shine a light. Get her in the morning. Plan ahead. Nothing like it. Her vagina; Shelly's cunt. When she orgasms it turns purple, deep purple like a monarch butterfly, then flutters into a hot, sweet pink. Like nothing you've ever seen.

WES. Sounds good.

BEN. You should get you some.

WES. She's not interested in me.

BEN. She could be.

WES. Yeah?

BEN. If you spend money on her, she'll come right around.

WES. Yeah.

BEN. My bet.

WES. How much would it take?

BEN. The less the better.

WES. Yeah?

BEN. She likes little things. Little thoughtful things.

WES. Like what?

BEN. A rubber duck for the bath. A plastic flower, so "it will never die." A barrette that has her name on it.

WES. If I don't get to fuck her, it won't be worth the trouble.

BEN. Trust me, I know.

WES. But she's in love with you.

BEN. Because of my thoughtfulness.

WES. Right. Yeah.

BEN. So be a little thoughtful.

WES. Why do women expect so much?

BEN. Because, I figured it out, it's because their fathers never loved them. Or maybe nobody ever loved them. But their fathers didn't for sure.

WES. Did you know her father?

BEN. I don't have to know the father, but I do know him.

WES. And he didn't love her?

BEN. No, I'm telling ya, that's basic. She was lucky he didn't kill her.

WES. And now I gotta, 'cause of him, I gotta buy this stuff. Be thoughtful.

BEN. Only if you want to get laid.

WES. Well, I do.

BEN. I figured.

WES. It just seems like … I mean, she's not buying me presents. Where's equal opportunity?

BEN. In your bad dreams.

WES. Well, it ain't fair.

BEN. What're you saying? You want a fucking rubber duck?

WES. No, but I'd like something. Maybe a pocket knife or something.

BEN. I'm seeing the Bradly in you, boy. That's your Bradly genes talking.

WES. Don't start in …

BEN. I wasn't but I will. I got the capabilities.

WES. Just 'cause Maw's down on 'em. Always talks down on 'em 'cause she's done so much better.

BEN. Living like a queen.

WES. Like to think she was. Won't help me out none. Tells me some days I'm not worth talking to 'cause I won't get a job and couldn't pass band and melted down all her food standing in front of the refrigerator. Even though she knows if I don't stay cool, I get this big rash. I guess it's my fault. I'm allergic to my own sweat. Nobody cares. Just let him scratch.

BEN. Look, here's five bucks, go get Shelly some fucking trinket

70

and let's see if she'll fuck you.

WES. Why're you helping me like this to fuck your girlfriend?

BEN. We don't know that she's my girlfriend. If she fucks you, she's not my girlfriend. Just a girl I fucked for trinkets and helped you to fuck too.

WES. *(Taking the money.)* I'm not good at picking presents.

BEN. Hey, I can't wipe your ass for you.

WES. I know.

BEN. You're nice looking. Stop acting like a loser.

WES. I'm not. I'm not.

BEN. Then go get her a present.

WES. I'm going.

BEN. I'm telling ya, you can do this.

WES. I know it. I know I can. One thing for sure, I look better than you.

BEN. So show me you can fuck her.

WES. I will. *(Wes exits stage left. Ben finishes his beer with the helpless gusto of the very lost and exits stage right. Shelly comes down center stage and sits on the bar stool. She carries a shoulder bag and wears a barrette with her name on it. She is sexy, in an old-fashioned, kittenish way. She sits on the stool, notices the static in her skirt, takes out Static Guard and sprays it. Wes enters with a brown sack.)* Hi, Shelly.

SHELLY. Oh! I was just ... my static.

WES. How ya doing?

SHELLY. Real good. Real good. Have you seen Ben?

WES. No.

SHELLY. He'll probably be here soon, ya think?

WES. I don't know.

SHELLY. He's mad at me.

WES. Yeah?

SHELLY. Uh-huh. Maybe.

WES. What'd you do?

SHELLY. I was dumb.

WES. Oh.

SHELLY. Don't tell anybody, but Ben made this pie, a lemon ice-box pie, and I think he squeezed in too many lemons or didn't remember how many eggs, because overnight it didn't gel. It just stayed real liquidy. And I said don't worry, we'll just say it's custard;

71

but he said it's supposed to be a pie. So we went on and took it to the Rodeo Picnic and set it out on the dessert table, and nobody ate it. I should of gone by and taken some pieces just to be nice, but there were all these other really good desserts: cherry cobbler, fudge brownies, homemade ice cream. At the Women's Crisis Center, they try to teach you it's healthier not to pretend to eat pie and secretly sling it in a trash barrel just to make somebody like you. But I think I'd be happier if Ben wasn't mad at me and I didn't feel like I was awfully mean and selfish not to even go by and take one piece of his pie. He worked hard making it. He wanted it to turn out good. It broke my heart because he pretended like it didn't matter when he came back and found out his was the only dessert on the whole table no one had even touched. I'm sorry I was talking fast, I been eating candy; I better shut up.

WES. *(After a beat.)* Hey, I got something for you.

SHELLY. You do?

WES. *(Giving her the sack.)* Here. *(Shelly opens the sack and takes out a small dime-store bottle of cologne.)*

SHELLY. Perfume.

WES. Yeah. It's a gift.

SHELLY. Tiger Rose. Thank you.

WES. Want to put some on?

SHELLY. Okay. *(She opens the bottle and smells.)* Mmm ... nice. *(She dabs the cologne on her wrists.)*

WES. Why ya putting it there?

SHELLY. When ya put it on the veins, the scent goes into the bloodstream and carries it over your whole body.

WES. *(Amazed.)* Huh.

SHELLY. *(Continuing to dab cologne.)* I also like t'put it behind my ears; so I can smell it. And back here on my neck so I smell good from behind. I mean all around.

WES. Uh-huh.

SHELLY. Thank you, Wes. I love presents.

WES. Glad you like it.

SHELLY. It's not my birthday or anything though.

WES. I know.

SHELLY. Why'd ya get it for me?

WES. I don't know. I thought you'd like it.

SHELLY. That's so thoughtful. That's so sweet.

WES. You're sweet.

SHELLY. No, I'm not.

WES. I think you are.

SHELLY. You do?

WES. I can't stop looking at that beauty mark you have.

SHELLY. Where?

WES. Right here on your neck.

SHELLY. That's just a mole. I might have to have it checked for cancer if it changes colors or grows a whole lot bigger.

WES. Looks like a beauty mark to me.

SHELLY. That's sweet.

WES. Shelly?

SHELLY. Yeah?

WES. You want me to buy you a beer?

SHELLY. Buy me a beer?! Wes, I swear, why are you being so sweet to me?

WES. I don't know. You deserve it.

SHELLY. No I don't.

WES. I think you do. How 'bout a beer?

SHELLY. All right, just one. Whatever they got on tap.

WES. Want some potato chips or pretzels?

SHELLY. Oh, stop it now! Just a beer, that's plenty.

WES. Be right back. *(He exits. She sits, lost and nervous for a moment, then looks down at the tiny bottle of cologne; her face glows.)*

Scene 7

LUNATIC, PART TWO

Sounds — hospital noises: sirens, gurneys being rolled, oxygen being pumped, x-rays being taken, doctors being paged, ominous drilling, etc. The Lunatic appears in a hospital gown. A shadow of bars falls across her. Time: Morning. Place: An asylum.

LUNATIC. I told them I only eat meat. Dog meat. Most people have something to say about that. Everyone wants to wag a finger. But I say "free country." No one ever argues with that. Although when you ask yourself "what's free about it?" ... the question is a stumper. You have to tell people what they want to hear or they don't come back. And so it is my lot to be a lunatic. Walking upright or on all fours, depending on the day and if I've been fed dog meat or snack packs. I would puke from it if they would allow me. I can't anymore. You see, it's this program. This no puking program. They want you to be fat. But you don't have to clean your plate. They don't force you to clean your plate. Imagine, making people eat. Making them keep it down. That's the part. Keeping it down. After meals, we have recreation and crafts. (She removes a large, damp, grey puzzle piece from her pocket.) I have a puzzle to solve. Pieces of piecemeal. Fragments; shards. It is all I can do to sit still and hold a grey section. Someone, I don't know who ... (but I could put on my thinking cap and guess) has mixed up the pieces and I'm very much afraid the Pastoral Scene and the Arc de Triomphe have been mixed up with the Jigsaw Mutant and Picasso's Guernica. Also to make things more unpleasant, someone ... (I wonder who?) has spilt cider over a big pile of pieces and the sticky ones got tossed out and are now lost for good. So this puzzle is a big mess. A big mess to take on. And, of course, there's a time limit, which has to be strictly enforced, but the rules are no

74

one knows for sure what it is. It varies for each player. That's how it's all kept fair. I'm sure though. I'm sure. As soon as I put everything together, all together, I'll be set free to leave. And I wonder when I leave where I should go first ... the porno store or the mall? Which would be more degrading?

Scene 8

LEAVING

Sounds: Haunting violin music that fades into a ceiling fan turning; a rocking chair creaking; a needle on a record that has stopped playing. Time: Late afternoon, as night is falling. Place: A decayed boudoir. The Grandmother, a sickly woman with one hand missing, lies on a chaise longue. Her Granddaughter sits next to her. Both wear half-masks. The Grandmother's mask is ancient, decadent and decayed. The Granddaughter's mask is defiantly neutral. They are both very still. A green-blue light washes over them. The Granddaughter brushes her Grandmother's hair. All of the movement in this scene should be choreographed in a stylized fashion.

GRANDDAUGHTER. Grandmother, will you tell me?
GRANDMOTHER. What?
GRANDDAUGHTER. Who was your lover that summer?
GRANDMOTHER. Which?
GRANDDAUGHTER. That summer you cut off your hand.
GRANDMOTHER. I put it in a velvet box and gave it away. A gift. Decorated with rings.
GRANDDAUGHTER. I wanted to know about it.
GRANDMOTHER. I've forgotten that story.
GRANDDAUGHTER. You said one day you would tell me.
GRANDMOTHER. Yes. I will. I'll tell.
GRANDDAUGHTER. *(Stops the brushing.)* I wanted to know.

GRANDMOTHER. Did they come? Did anyone come?

GRANDDAUGHTER. Not yet.

GRANDMOTHER. When are they expected?

GRANDDAUGHTER. They've sent regrets.

GRANDMOTHER. All of them?

GRANDDAUGHTER. Yes.

GRANDMOTHER. They've responded?

GRANDDAUGHTER. Yes.

GRANDMOTHER. No one is coming?

GRANDDAUGHTER. They sent regrets.

GRANDMOTHER. Finally then. Get my jewels. I want to wear some of them. *(The Granddaughter gets the Grandmother's jewels and opens the case.)* Beautiful.

GRANDDAUGHTER. Yes.

GRANDMOTHER. *(Pointing to an opulent necklace.)* That one.

GRANDDAUGHTER. Yes. *(She takes out the necklace and puts it on her Grandmother.)* Grandmother? Tell me something.

GRANDMOTHER. I don't know anything.

GRANDDAUGHTER. My father. Your son. What was he like?

GRANDMOTHER. I don't remember.

GRANDDAUGHTER. Please.

GRANDMOTHER. He didn't take care of his teeth.

GRANDDAUGHTER. Ah.

GRANDMOTHER. *(Pointing to a jeweled bracelet.)* This one.

GRANDDAUGHTER. Yes.

GRANDMOTHER. *(Lifting her twisted hand very slowly, wearing the heavy bracelet.)* My hand. It mortifies me with its stillness. It's hard not to feel self-pity when your fingers are too withered to wear rings. Lovely rings. Such a collection. *(About the case of jewels.)* Take that away.

GRANDDAUGHTER. Yes. *(The Granddaughter removes the jeweled case.)*

GRANDMOTHER. You have always been my favorite.

GRANDDAUGHTER. I know.

GRANDMOTHER. Of course I loved them all. They may not have known it. But they were all loved. Will you tell them?

GRANDDAUGHTER. Yes.

GRANDMOTHER. They won't believe you.

GRANDDAUGHTER. No.

GRANDMOTHER. Then don't. Don't then. Don't tell them. *(The light has slowly changed to a deep blue-green.)* It frightens me.

GRANDDAUGHTER. What?

GRANDMOTHER. The light. How it changes, this time of day, when it begins to get dark. Give me the medicine.

GRANDDAUGHTER. Now?

GRANDMOTHER. Yes. Be a good girl.

GRANDDAUGHTER. Yes. *(The Granddaughter takes a brown bottle from the bedside table. She pours into a teaspoon.)*

GRANDMOTHER. Careful, don't spill.

GRANDDAUGHTER. No. *(The Granddaughter gives her Grandmother the spoonful of liquid.)*

GRANDMOTHER. Done.

GRANDDAUGHTER. Yes.

GRANDMOTHER. I feel good now. Better.

GRANDDAUGHTER. All I want … I just want to know. That summer, your lover, who was he?

GRANDMOTHER. Look in the drawer, you'll find what I've left you. A remembrance. *(The Granddaughter opens a drawer in the bedside table. She takes out a limp red balloon.)* Don't take it outside to play. It's dangerous. If you swallow the rubber, you could choke on it and die. Play with it in here.

GRANDDAUGHTER. All right. *(She begins pulling on the balloon.)* Grandmother. Do you believe in anything?

GRANDMOTHER. Yes, I do. Of course I do.

GRANDDAUGHTER. What is it?

GRANDMOTHER. Sophistry.

GRANDDAUGHTER. Ah.

GRANDMOTHER. Blow up the balloon.

GRANDDAUGHTER. Yes. *(She starts blowing up the balloon and then stops.)* Grandmother, one more thing.

GRANDMOTHER. I'm tired now.

GRANDDAUGHTER. Please. Who was he? *(She continues to blow up the balloon.)*

GRANDMOTHER. A red balloon.

GRANDDAUGHTER. Who was your lover that summer? *(She blows slowly into the balloon.)* Try to remember.

GRANDMOTHER. I've given you the balloon. *(The Grandmother quietly dies. The Granddaughter sucks air from the balloon, blows it back in, sucks it out, blows it back.)*
GRANDDAUGHTER. If only you could tell me something, something. Please. *(Air rushes from the balloon, which shrivels in her hand.)* Something that you know. *(The lights turn blue, violet, red, black.)*

Scene 9

LEARNER, PART TWO

Sounds: Branches whacking against windowpanes; howling winds; water boiling. Time: A snowy winter night. Place: The Learner's garret apartment. A pinlight illuminates the Learner's bony hand as it picks ball of lint from his trousers.

LEARNER. Lucheea. Poem. Lucheea. Poem. Poem. Poem. Poem. *(The lights brighten, and we find the Learner lying on his side with a pensive look on his face.)* In trying to use my brain ... in trying to use my brain, I find there are gaps. I lie on my side wearing black trousers with hairs that arrived from I know not where, clinging to the fabric, giving me something to ponder and pick. Progress is eventually made and the pants have less straying hair but, strangely enough, there are always some. Lucheea. Poem. Lucheea. Poem. And, by the way, there's food as well on the pants. Old food on the clothes. Why don't you toss them in the laundry? Do a load. I'll have to go to the laundromat. It's snowing in Urbana tonight. Better put on your galoshes. Galoshes. Haven't had galoshes since the fifth grade. They were yellow and they're gone. I could put paper bags around my feet. Tie them with string, rope, tape ... walk out in the snow; walk out in the snow ... Is there no idea!? No idea that will come to me? Lucheea. Poem. Lucheea. Snow. Lucheea.

Such a beautiful name. Are you a true dunce, a complete fool

78

that nothing comes to you? Nothing flows forth? The sound alone. La, la, la. El. The sound of L alone ... Let's do some research. *(He picks up a mammoth dictionary.)* Scholars often do, do research. A common practice among them. Here we have it. The L's ... Look. All of these words. Loaves of them, loaves of them. Labyrinth, lack, larceny, lark, lassitude, lacerate, lorn, liquescent. Lost, loser, lethargy, let, liberation, light, liquescent. Liar, life, lobotomy, load, lubricate, loyalty, lupine, liquescent ...

L-words. Limitless. They are limitless. Yet there is a limit. You have a unifying element. A pattern in the universe, something to hang your hat on — the heartbeat of the L.

And it comes to me. An idea. An idea as big as candy in the hands of children. As big as the miracle that is spring.

Loneliness, linked, loser, lunatic, learner, leaving, lost, life, love, life, lost, love, life ...

Scene 10

LIFE

Sounds: Drumbeat, heartbeat, falling water, vague distant chant — "life, life, life, life" etc. Time: Dawn of man. Place: Earth. We hear the narrator's amplified voice but do not see him.

NARRATOR. There once were three Ones. A Big One, a Middle One, and a Small One. *(The Ones emerge each from their own hole. The Ones are covered with dark mud. Their facial features are high-lighted with rich earth colors.)* They were at large together. *(The Ones circle each other, dazed and stupefied, staring at various body parts of their own and each other.)* But they were bored and boring Ones. They never celebrated occasions and failed to share or savor the moment or even bare their teeth and indulge in inappropriate behavior. *(The Ones stop and stare dumbly at the ground, shuffling their feet.)* Then one day the Ones were given a gift. *(A fanfare. The*

Shoe enters, dressed in black, decorated with a dazzling red shoestring and a crisp white tongue. The Shoe soft-shoes around the stage.) The gift was a big shoe. The Ones were primitive beings and they did not know the beginnings about a thing such as a shoe. The Shoe was a shy shoe and was at a loss as to how to please six feet. *(The Shoe soft-shoes around the Ones. The Ones are confused and horrified. They scatter and regroup, surrounding the Shoe with menace.)*

The Big One decided they must build a cage for the Shoe. *(The Big One pulls down a web of string and, with the help of the others, surrounds the perplexed Shoe.)* The Shoe objected. Things got uglier and uglier. And finally the shoe was tied up. *(The Shoe is wrapped in the web and, though it tries to escape, cannot. The Big One swaggers, bangs its chest and yells out guttural cries of victory. The other two Ones stand by and watch, nodding their heads, impressed.)* The Big One decided the Shoe would be butchered at daybreak. *(The Big One acts out the butchery of the trembling Shoe. The other Ones are ignited by this passion.)* Blood lust was in the air. Wild revelry ensued. *(Music plays. The three Ones do a dance of blood lust.)* Inappropriate behavior abounded. *(The dance builds to animalistic debauchery.)* Sleep descended to quell the raging blood of the Ones. *(The lights dim, and the spent Ones return to their holes to sleep.)* The Shoe felt heartsick and sighed. Moonlight shuddered at the ache of the sound. And the Small One awoke. *(The Shoe twists itself with grotesque anguish and cries out. The night lights shimmer. The Small One comes out of its hole and approaches the caged Shoe.)*

The Shoe looked at the Small One and smiled in an attempt to break the ice. The Little One had never seen a smile and was frightened. *(The small One cowers. The Shoe laughs and yelps. The Small One becomes angry and tortures the Shoe in its cage. The Shoe cries. The Small One is amazed to see such a thing as tears and reaches into the Shoe's cage to touch and taste the tears. The Small One likes the bitter taste and attempts to get more tears. The Shoe kicks the Small One and comes out of its cage. The Small One cries. The Shoe struts some, then thinks better of it and gives the Small One comfort. The Shoe kisses the Small One with many soft, quick kisses. The Small One is bedazzled and quickly kisses the Shoe, then begins to giggle with high-pitched delight. The Shoe and the Small One roll around the stage laughing themselves sick.)*

Suddenly, the Middle One awoke to the noise. *(The Middle One comes out of its hole and gestures to the Small One with severe displeasure. The Small One scampers back to its hole.)* The Middle One commanded the Shoe return to its cage. *(The Middle One stops, wags its arms at the Shoe and bellows. The Shoe gives it a surly grin.)* The Shoe was feeling frisky out in the night air under the stars. The Shoe wanted to dance. *(Music plays. The Shoe dances elegantly around the stage, then extends a hand to the Middle One, imploring it to join. The Middle One folds its arms around its head.)* The Shoe produced a bright yellow branch and touched the Middle One's heart with it. *(The Middle One sighs a sigh so strange we cannot begin to fathom where it comes from. The Shoe uses the yellow branch to conduct the Middle One in a mysterious, beautiful dance. The Middle One dances across the forest elated. The Shoe joins the Middle One in the enchanted dance. A burst of red stars explodes across the sky.)* Never having danced, it was a great occasion for the Middle One, who fell in love with Shoe and wanted to save it from all harm forever. *(The Middle One caresses the Shoe, begging it to run and escape. They twist together and claw apart, trying to discover which direction they should go. Daylight begins to break. The Big One stirs. The Middle One panics at the rumblings of the Big One and takes the Shoe by its tongue, twists it and pulls it off in the direction of day.)*

Daybreak arrived. The Big One awoke with the swell of blood in its mouth. *(The Big One comes out of its hole slurping and rolling its head. It looks to the Middle One's hole and finds it is empty. The Big One rushes to the Shoe's cage and frantically searches through the empty web. Covered in the spidery net, the Big One rages back and forth, bellowing in disbelief. The Small One appears from its hole, wiping sleep from its eyes.)* There was nothing to do but ransack the Small One. *(The Big One pummels the Small One, beating it nearly to death. The Small One lies gasping for breath. The Big One is chilled by a dreadful moment of despair and self-loathing. It goes to the Small One and kicks it gently. The Small One pleads for mercy. The Big One wraps the Small One up in the web, picks it up and carries it off through the woods.)*

Meanwhile, the Shoe and the Middle One have danced themselves ragged, past lust and to the bone. *(The Shoe and the Middle One appear. They show distinct signs of exhaustion and decay. The branch the Shoe holds is no longer bright yellow; it has turned blood-brown.)* Too many nights under the stars can burn you. *(The Shoe looks at the Middle One and haphazardly waves the branch. The Middle One gives an uninspired wag of its foot. The Shoe shrugs as if to say, "not bad")*

One day they fought over a trifle. *(The Shoe motions for the Middle One to go ahead. The Middle One defers and motions to the Shoe, "It's okay, you go ahead." The Shoe declines, insistently giving the right of way to the Middle One. The Middle One declines, and so forth until wild gesturing erupts. A poke and a shove follow. Then a series of horrible huffs.)* But later they blamed it all on the location of the moon. *(The Shoe and the Middle One begin shrugging their shoulders. The Middle One points out the moon with the branch. They both nod in agreement and shake their heads at the moon in disgust. The Middle One breaks the branch across its knee and slings part of it off into the woods. They exit aimlessly.)*

And, on the other side of things, the Big One and the Small One felt a loss. *(The Big One and Small One enter side by side. They come stage center and stare out across the audience.)* They knew that they must search for the Middle One. *(The Big One turns and the Small One follows. They circle around the stage in a plodding manner.)* Although most of the time they felt their search was useless. *(They stop and circle in the opposite direction, then exit. The Middle One enters stage right, chewing on the half branch that is now white with age.)* Secretly, the Middle One felt a loss but told no one. *(The Shoe enters stage left slumped with despair. The Shoe and the Middle One stop center stage and stare at one another.)*

The Shoe was heartsick and wanted to leave. *(The Shoe holds out its hand for the Middle One to shake. The Middle One covers its mouth with its hands. The Shoe waves farewell. The Middle One puts the stick in its mouth and falls to the ground, bereft.)* A horrible loss of dignity ensued. *(The Middle One silently rolls around the stage with the stick in its mouth. Finally, it stops at the Shoe's feet. The Shoe sadly pats the head of the Middle One.)* It was decided that the Shoe would stay. *(The Middle One and the Shoe sit together but apart. Eventually, the Middle One takes the stick out of its mouth and jabs it into its heart; the Shoe winces with untold anguish.)*

One day the Small One appeared. *(The Small One enters and*

begins to amuse the Shoe with strange antics, such as quick little kisses and flapping its arms as wings. The Shoe responds, and they begin to play together.) Then came the Big One. (The Big One enters with a giant jagged sword. Sounds of drums beating, violins scraping. The oppressive shadows of prehistoric birds fall chaotically across the stage. The Small One moves away from the Shoe. The Middle One does a fierce, stylized dance to barricade the Big One from the Shoe. The Big One looks at the Middle One, gestures majestically, then freezes in a horrific pose that both demands and begs. The Middle One steps aside.) And the Big One cut the Shoe to shreds, while the Small One laughed with a horror that filled the forest, and the Middle One watched silently and smiled a sick smile. (The Big One takes the knife and viciously rips the Shoe to shreds. Cries of wild animals and human infants.) It was a ghastly occurrence. And ended unceremoniously. (The Shoe dies. The Big One cuts off steaming parts of the Shoe and hands them to the others. They eat the victuals, blood dripping from their mouths.) The three Ones looked at each other baring their blood-caked teeth. (Music plays. The three Ones circle each other, baring their crimson teeth.) They knew they had been through something. A bright yellow branch. Branch. Yellow branch. A branch. Yellow branch. (White stars ignite the sky. Fade out.)

Scene 11

LUNATIC, PART THREE

Time: Now. Place: Here. Piped organ merry-go-round music plays. The Lunatic appears in a tattered circus dress with a full net skirt. A worn pouch hangs from her waist. One of her legs is missing. She hobbles haltingly on bright-colored crutches.

LUNATIC. It was a setback. A minor setback. Often they occur. Uh-oh! There's no more milk in the refrigerator! I'll have to eat my cereal dry.

Trash day! Trash day! Look who didn't put out any garbage cans!

And then there are other more severe setbacks. Like the mop to the nose, waking up with fruit, or believing your leg is filling up with rat-dirty-water-excrement, and you try to hack it off with garden clippers but the thigh bone, the femur, is too thick. And ugly complications arise.

Later you have to learn to walk on crutches, which is harder than it looks.

Setbacks can eat up your life.

It's best to be prepared for emergencies. I have a pouch full of emergency equipment: candy, tweezers, stuffed toy, silk panties, razor blades, can opener, family picture, maps of places, canteen, Vaseline, keys, roundabouts, clean socks, a daily calendar, and valentine. At one time there were Tic-Tacs, but they disappeared. Guess who? *(A pause.)*

You have to tell people what they want to hear or they don't come back.

You have to tell people ... you have to tell ... you have to tell ... tell people ... tell people ... tell ... tell ... tell. *(Pretending to write in the air.)*

Dear Blank, Blank. I'm feeling now ... feeling now ... like I am circling the pit. A final walk on the rim. *(She circles around the stage on her crutches.)*

Look Maw, no hands! No hands to grab, to save, to wave, to blow a kiss goodbye.

How long does my solo act last? I appreciate the space you've given me to fill on this bill, but are there no other performers? No one to share the finale with? *(A long beat, filled with a horribly sweet need and loneliness.)*

Accentuate the positive. Accentuate the positive.

Open space is a wonderful asset. A miracle of possibilities.

And my life is completely empty. Wheat fields of emptiness.

Like a vacant ballroom waiting for whatever I choose.

Waltzes and champagne, sardines on crackers and the theme of the ball will be everyone must wear green and whisper secrets into strangers' ears. And the stories that are told will be revealed at midnight, and prizes will be given. And no one, no one, no one will ever leave empty-handed. *(A spotlight hits the Lunatic. A waltz plays.*

She twirls around the stage on her crutches, then comes to a stop.)
When will they arrive, I wonder? All the guests? My company? I must prepare: invitations are to be sent; food will be cooked; decorations; musicians. Yes, good, good, good. I smell the smell of … fresh baked bread. Fresh baked bread from the kitchen.

The kitchen? Where's the kitchen? Has there always been a kitchen? *(Desperately, she seeks to follow the scent. The trail leads her higher and higher. Finally, she is sniffing upwards, her nose high in the air. From above, warm, friendly kitchen sounds: wooden spoons mixing batter in bowls; oven doors opening and closing; water running; lettuce being torn; soft, friendly voices chattering.)*

Oh. Oh. Oh. Ah, up there.

It's very true. I do not look up enough. I do not raise my head and eyes to look at the sky. Note its color, the time of day, the weather conditions. I do not look up enough. I have always been more comfortable with a bowed head. *(Sniffing as she gazes upward.)*

Pumpkin bread. Beef stew. A bowl of apples. How I'm looking forward to supper tonight. Supper with the others up there in the kitchen.

Scene 12

LEARNER, PART THREE

Time: Now. Place: College campus. a pinlight comes up on the Learner's hand, holding a crumpled sheet of paper on which a poem is written.

LEARNER. Today in class my L-poem was read. *(The lights come up as the Learner walks toward the audience, uncrumpling the paper.)* If one were to believe in the grading system of a third-rate university, then we would have our conclusions drawn for us. *(Reading.)* "The concept of your poem is, to say the least, absurd. To write a poem based on the letter L suggests an immature nature found suspect beyond the age of three. "Daddy, don't you think eights are better than twos? Blue's my favorite color. I bet rhinoceroses are the biggest animals ... " Etcetera, etcetera and so forth.

D plus. The plus is nice. Plus what? Plus pity? Plus pain? Plus pustules?

But I wholly reject and disregard this classification. Nothing is not minute enough to describe what it means to me.

It is she. She. Lucheea. Who held my grade. Held it in her eyes (brown her eyes.).

When my poem was read. She did not cry like with Proofrock. But chewed cow-like on a red pencil. Teeth tapping innocuously on the eraserless tool. Her brown eyes floating across the fluorescent ceiling, lost in private reverie. Unchanged by my bon mots, heart's surges, brain struggles, soul's pourings. After class I went up to her ... (*Lucheea, a beautiful young girl with auburn hair, appears. She carries a tower of books, effortlessly.*) Was it tasty?

LUCHEEA. What?

LEARNER. The pencil? The red one?

LUCHEEA. Sorry, I don't have an extra pencil.

LEARNER. Well, I don't need one. I have many pens.

LUCHEEA. Oh.

LEARNER. I wanted to ask you about my poem.

LUCHEEA. The one heard in class today?

LEARNER. Yes. That one. What did you think? I want an honest reaction. There's no point in not being utterly frank. Speak what your heart tells you.

LUCHEEA. I didn't know where it was going.

LEARNER. Oh no, of course not. Certainly I planned that. Any other remarks?

LUCHEEA. It made me think ... of other things.

LEARNER. Right. Good. (*A beat.*) May I help you with your books?

LUCHEEA. I haven't got that many today. Thanks all the same. (*Lucheea exits.*)

LEARNER. And so she was gone, walking down the hall with her skyload of books.

And I kept watching her, waiting for her to trip. Trip with all of those books and bruise up her knees and elbows and cry like a little girl thrown out on the pavement.

But she kept on walking, a shaft of light across her. On out the door where sunlight gallantly burst through her auburn hair.

And I felt sick with ... sick from ... the trail of her smell. And I knew I would excavate all the ... every tomb of the alphabet to discover ... in search ... eternal search of the word, the letter, the breath that would please her. *(Hold a moment. Blackout. Music plays. Perhaps Dean Martin singing "That's Amoré"*)*

End of Play

---

* See Special Note on Songs and Recordings on copyright page.

PROPERTY LIST

Bottle of sherry
Large white handkerchief
Beer bottles
Phone (MONICA)
Gun (PRICE)
Torn grocery bag, pen (JAY)
Invitation (MALCOLM)
Slim volume (LEARNER)
$5 bill (BEN)
Shoulder bag, barrette, Static Guard (SHELLEY)
Brown sack with cologne bottle (WES)
Large soggy grey puzzle piece (LUNATIC)
Half-masks (GRANDMOTHER, GRANDDAUGHTER)
Hairbrush (GRANDMOTHER, GRANDDAUGHTER)
Jewel case, necklace, bracelet (GRANDMOTHER,
     GRANDDAUGHTER)
Brown bottle of medicine, teaspoon (GRANDDAUGHTER)
Limp red balloon (GRANDDAUGHTER)
Ball of lint (LEARNER)
Big dictionary (LEARNER)
Web of string (BIG ONE)
Yellow branch (SHOE)
Blood-brown branch (SHOE)
White half-branch (MIDDLE ONE)
Knife (BIG ONE)
Pouch, crutches (LUNATIC)
Crumpled sheet of paper (LEARNER)
Books (LUCHEEA)

SOUND EFFECTS

Winter winds, distant train, dogs barking, church bells
Gunshot
Back alley sounds, flamenco music, infant crying, cat screeching
Hacking cough
Urban street sounds
Knocking
Loud bells clanging
People partying
Flatulent sounds
Daytime TV shows
Flies swarming and being swatted
Poolhall sounds: pinball machine, beers sliding down bar, country
   jukebox
Hospital noises
Haunting violin music, ceiling fan, rocking chair, broken record
Branches hitting window, wind, water boiling
Drumbeat, heartbeat, falling water, chant
Heartbeat
Voice
Music
Cries of wild animals and infants
Merry-go-round music
Waltz
Kitchen sounds

SISTERS OF
THE WINTER
MADRIGAL

SISTERS OF THE WINTER MADRIGAL was produced by Rolling Pictures in association with Moving Arts (Julie Briggs and Lee Wochner, Artistic Directors) in 2001. It was directed by Frederick Bailey; the set design was by Victoria Profitt; the sound and music design were by Sean Murray; the costume design was by Atsuko Ohtani Bailey; and the stage managers were Donnetta Grays and Alma Carrasco. The cast was as follows:

CALAIH .... Cerris Morgan-Moyer
STEPHAN .... Kris Kamm
ALEXTON .... Cris D'Annunzio
TARETTA .... Naomi Chan
MARDIAN .... Camilla Carr
APOTHECARY .... Valeri Ross
HIGH LORD .... Tim Woodward
LETTER WRITER .... Darrell Kunitomi
BLACKSMITH .... Rudy Young
2 GUARDS .... Darrell Kunitomi
Rudy Young

CHARACTERS

CALAIH

STEPHAN

ALEXTON

TARETTA

MARDIAN

APOTHECARY

HIGH LORD

LETTER WRITER

BLACKSMITH

2 GUARDS

PLACE and TIME

Long ago in a land far away.

SISTERS OF THE WINTER MADRIGAL

Scene 1

At night in the early autumn by the stream and hillside. Calaih stands onstage holding a thin stick, waiting. She is small with a plain face, but she has beautiful red hair that reaches almost to the ground.

Stephan, a tall young man, enters. He tosses pebbles into the stream. Calaih moves closer to Stephan and breaks the stick in two. He turns to see her.

STEPHAN. Oh, it is you. *(They stare at each other.)* You are a strange girl. And yet they say the High Lord sent you a silver brush and comb for your long red hair. They say he is in love with you. I would use the word enchanted or fascinated or even curious myself. For I feel it is an impossibility to love someone with whom you have never even spoken. Where is your cow?

CALAIH. Eating grass up on the hill.

STEPHAN. Oh, so you do talk indeed. You must excuse me but so often I see you walking with your cow and I offer greetings and you say nothing, or you will come into my father's shop only to stare in silence and eat cheese while I laugh and tell stories as I work. Oh, there are times when you will come and hold your torn boots in your arms and nod up and down at my father — but never will you speak or smile or nod with me. Why can you not be like your sister, she is gay with every man. Excuse me. I regret mentioning it. There is nothing to be concerned about, Calaih.

CALAIH. The reason I do not speak to you is that I become

timid. Do you know I walk up the hill and down again stamping over the sharpest rocks and stones only so my boots will be in need of repair and I may go to the shoemaker's shop to see you telling stories and laughing. My cow and me, we come here every night and stand on the hill to watch you sitting by this stream looking at the stars.

STEPHAN. You watch me here at night?

CALAIH. *(Nods.)* And sometimes you throw rocks.

STEPHAN. I did not know that — I thought at times you must be —

CALAIH. What?

STEPHAN. Haughty.

CALAIH. Haughty?

STEPHAN. *(Nods.)* Because — because of your long fine hair and the gifts the High Lord sent to you and your quietness — to me, and because of my fondness for you ... I like to watch you eating cheese.

CALAIH. Do you love me then?

STEPHAN. Yes.

CALAIH. Good. *(She goes and kisses him.)*

STEPHAN. I must go now ...

CALAIH. Why do you go then?

STEPHAN. My love is too deep.

CALAIH. Please, you must love me in this soft grass, under the night stars. For I have loved you so long, Stephan the Shoemaker's Son.

STEPHAN. Oh, Calaih, Orphan of Joshua the Cow Herder. You will get sticks and berries in your soft hair.

CALAIH. Please, hold me. Hold me. It is cool here tonight. *(They hold each other in the grass as the lights fade.)*

Scene 2

The same autumn night in Taretta's room above the tavern. Taretta is an attractive, sensual woman with dark hair and violet eyes. She sits at her dressing table rubbing cream on her arms and hands. She is wearing a beautiful, seductive robe. Alexton's voice is heard from outside.

ALEXTON'S VOICE. Taretta. It is I.

TARETTA. *(Picking up mirror.)* Come in, Alexton. *(Alexton enters. He looks like a goose. He stands at the entrance nervously, holding a box.)* I will be ready in a minute. You may get undressed if you like.

ALEXTON. Oh, very well. *(He undresses throughout the following segments.)* I am glad you picked me tonight. I needed your company. My wife is a dowdy woman. This evening she went outside and sat in the garden dirt and cried.

TARETTA. Yes, she is a very dowdy woman. Why did you marry her?

ALEXTON. My life is sick and sad, Taretta. Without the sweet favors you bestow on me, I would be dead.

TARETTA. Tell me, do you think the High Lord would wish to lie with me? Do you think he would enjoy being ravished by Taretta, Woman of Flaming Nights? That is how Heilington describes me — the Woman of Flaming Nights.

ALEXTON. Do not speak of Heilington. This is my time with you, Taretta. Do not speak of any of the others. Let them sit downstairs listening to your cries and shrieks knowing I am with you. Let them sit there and drown their sorrows alone, as I have done so many nights.

TARETTA. Ah, poor Alexton.

ALEXTON. Do not take any others tonight, Taretta. Let me be the only one.

TARETTA. If you can satisfy me, I will not. Now — shall I take

97

off my robe? *(He nods. She removes robe and stands before him in seductive undergarments.)*

ALEXTON. Here are the gifts I bring you. One gold fan. A piece of silk brought from my store. Two jeweled earbobs. A purple rock.

TARETTA. What is this? A rock? What do I want with a rock, Alexton?

ALEXTON. It is a purple rock. I found it by the stream. The purple is like that purple in your eyes, my dearest Taretta.

TARETTA. I have no use for a rock. *(He takes it back.)*

ALEXTON. Here is something you will like. *(He presents a headdress.)*

TARETTA. Lovely, very lovely. It will look well with my autumn gown. But I have seen this somewhere before … I have seen it before indeed. This is your wife's headdress. She wore it only last week at the autumn festival with a very unsuitable gown. She will recognize this if I wear it.

ALEXTON. I do not care. It suits you — not her.

TARETTA. Yes, but she will beat your children and your dog with a stick.

ALEXTON. And I will beat her with a limb off of the cypress tree. Wear it, I beg you … wear it alone with nothing and this gold is yours. *(He holds up money pouch. She places on the headdress.)* I will leave my dog with my brother. I do not want to have him beaten again.

Scene 3

Early the next morning at the two sisters' cottage. Calaih sits at the table, brushing sticks and grass and berries out of her hair and eating cheese. Taretta enters, with a box of gifts and bags of money.

TARETTA. Good morning, sister.
CALAIH. Good morning.

TARETTA. Where is your cow?

CALAIH. Outside. He is lying in the sun.

TARETTA. I had quite an evening last night. *(Dropping box and bags on table.)* Look at what Alexton has given me. There is a gold fan in there, silk from his shop, jeweled earbobs, and even his wife's autumn headdress. Here are the gold and coins I have gotten. This much from just Alexton alone; the rest is from all the others.

CALAIH. *(Touching the piece of silk.)* That is nice.

TARETTA. *(She begins counting money.)* Soon I will be leaving this hovel. I will get me a beautiful home near all the shops around the square. I have those debts left to pay on those new jewels and gowns, then I will be gone. Would you pour me some milk? My arm is aching.

CALAIH. *(Pouring milk.)* Here.

TARETTA. *(Drinking milk.)* You know, you are not so plain, Calaih. The High Lord even sent you that silver brush and comb. There is no reason for you to be poor. That is fifty there. But perhaps your appetites are not as developed as mine. I who can satisfy any man in any way. That makes seventy-five. But I will tell you a secret: Though these men are thoroughly nourished through my skills and charms. Ninety. There remains within me a deep craving. Do you understand that? As if one could pour hot gold into me for an eternity. And it would not be enough. A hundred there. But you do not understand. Though the High Lord sends you gifts, you could not meet his needs as I could. Ah, that makes one hundred and six. What a night. *(She begins raking money into her purse.)*

CALAIH. I am in love with Stephan the Shoemaker's Son, Taretta. This morning he walked me home with my cow, and he talked to us and petted my cow. He said, "This is a very fine cow you have." Then he said my name, "Calaih." Like that he said it, "Calaih."

TARETTA. Stephan the Shoemaker's son. That strange boy? The one who always has a joke for you? *(Calaih nods.)* I have always thought him a noodle. He will never be a rich man. But if you love him — if you love this noodle —

CALAIH. You need not mock Stephan. He is dear to me and of greater worth than any of the baggage you have had.

TARETTA. You speak in jealousy, Little Calf. *(Mardian, an older woman with purple lips, enters. There are two guards behind her.)*

99

MARDIAN. Good morning. I am Mardian, Social Messenger to the High Lord. May I come in?

TARETTA. Yes. Come in.

MARDIAN. So you are Calaih, Orphan of Joshua the Cow Herder. You hair is as lovely as they say. May I touch it? *(She feels Calaih's hair.)* Now here is the proclamation I am to read to you. "Notice to all the Subjects. The High Lord proclaims he shall take Calaih, Orphan of Joshua the Cow Herder, as his Wife and High Lady. The ceremony is to take place on the last night of late winter. Only the bride and Special Attendants to the High Lord are to be allowed at the ceremony. However, there will be a public celebration the following morning on the first day of spring." *(Noticing Calaih's unenthusiastic reaction.)* Do you not understand this proclamation, Calaih, Orphan of Joshua the Cow Herder?

CALAIH. I am to marry the High Lord on the last night of late winter.

MARDIAN. Yes, you have understood it well. How bright you are. And such fine hair. This proclamation shall now be taken to the Great Wall where all will read it and envy you your good fortune.

TARETTA. Wait. Are you certain there is no mistake?

MARDIAN. Mistake?

TARETTA. In the proclamation.

MARDIAN. There is no mistake, Taretta, Orphan Whore of Joshua the Cow Herder. Good day now. *(Mardian and the Guards exit.)*

TARETTA. So. I suppose you can gloat over this proclamation. You with your fine silver brush and comb.

CALAIH. What does the High Lord look like? Is he old or young?

TARETTA. Older than you — but not so old.

CALAIH. Do you remember the woman he set on fire?

TARETTA. Yes, Della — that ugly whore.

CALAIH. I remember how her flesh dripped off like thin wax and she was crying. I heard her crying coming from the flames.

TARETTA. Della — What an eyesore to the town she was, with her pox-marked face and hunched shoulders. They could burn all her kind for all I would care. Where are you going?

CALAIH. Outside, to sit with my cow. *(Calaih exits.)*

TARETTA. Very well. Go outside and sit with your cow. I am tired. My arm aches. *(She sits rubbing her hand and arm.)*

Scene 4

Afternoon, in the middle of winter, in the Apothecary's treatment room.

APOTHECARY. *(Finishing mixing his potion.)* The preparation is complete. Come in when you are ready. The wind is cold. I will have to put mortar in these cracks. *(Takes bandages out.)* Tell me about the wedding plans. How is it to have your sister betrothed to the High Lord? *(Taretta enters, with her arm covered in a cloth.)*
TARETTA. I pay you money, Apothecary, I expect a cure. Look at my arm; the bumps have grown. They are darker now and hard. At times I cannot move my arm for the pain it causes.
APOTHECARY. My potion soothes your pain, does it not, Taretta? *(Dips bandages into potion.)*
TARETTA. For a time, that is all, for a time.
APOTHECARY. Take down the cloth now. *(She does so, and the Apothecary begins wrapping hot bandages around her arm. She flinches in pain.)* There. Think of something else for a moment and the burning will subside. Tell me about the wedding plans. How is it to have your sister betrothed to the High Lord?
TARETTA. Do not speak of it. It is of no use to me. My arm is burning. I tell you I cannot bear it. Take it off.
APOTHECARY. Here, lie back now. Lie back and breathe. *(She lies back, breathing heavily.)* It is already the middle of winter. Just think, little Calaih will soon be moving to the castle of the High Lord.
TARETTA. Damn you; I said not to speak of it.
APOTHECARY. Very well, Taretta. *(The Apothecary begins putting up potion and bandages. Taretta lies back, taking deep breaths.)*
TARETTA. Tell me, Apothecary — you have not told, have you? I pay you well to keep your mouth shut.
APOTHECARY. I have not told.
TARETTA. Some of the men — they do not come anymore. They are not the same with me when I tell them I wear red velvet

on my arm as they do in France, for the alluring … to be alluring.
You do not tell them of my visits, Apothecary?
APOTHECARY. No.
TARETTA. Good. They must not find out. They must always
fight to come to me. They must always want and love me.
APOTHECARY. You can get dressed now, Taretta. Pay me my fee
and go home.
TARETTA. Yes. I will get dressed. One minute and I will get up
and get dressed.

Scene 5

*At night in midwinter by the stream and hillside. Calaih sits
wrapped in a thick shawl, despondently breaking sticks. Stephan
enters carrying a satchel. She looks up at him and gasps.*

STEPHAN. Where is your cow?
CALAIH. Down by the stream, licking stones in the water.
STEPHAN. You are always with your cow.
CALAIH. Where have you been? I go to the shop every day and
ask for you, but they do not tell me where you have gone. I wait
here with my cow every night in the cold. We look for you to
come — but you do not come. Where have you been?
STEPHAN. I have been away — on a journey. Why do you cry?
CALAIH. Because I am so stupid. After that one night I thought
you loved me, but then the next morning you go away.
STEPHAN. Calaih, I am no fool. That morning I saw the
proclamation. You are to be wedded to the High Lord. He has
sought you out and will give you finery and you will live in rich
comfort and your children can eat gold every morning for breakfast if they wish. You will be happy.
CALAIH. You believe that riches would make me so happy? That
I would want all this gold and jewels and riches. I would scratch
off the flesh from the High Lord's face. I would stab out the eyes

102

of those fat children eating gold, if only you would not believe I would be wedded for riches.

STEPHAN. I am sorry. I know you would not be.

CALAIH. Tell me —

STEPHAN. What?

CALAIH. Do you want me?

STEPHAN. Yes.

CALAIH. For a wife?

STEPHAN. Yes.

CALAIH. I will go tell my cow.

STEPHAN. Calaih, wait! You cannot marry me. It will be against the proclamation. I will not see you hurt.

CALAIH. He will not hurt me. He does not love me. He thinks my hair is beautiful. He sends a silver comb and brush saying, "For your beautiful long red hair, I worship it." What a noodle to worship hair. If he loves my hair, I will chop it off and send it to him in a box. But he shall not have me. I will go to the Letter Writer and have him send a message to the High Lord. I will say kindly that I cannot marry him as I am betrothed to Stephan the Shoemaker's Son.

STEPHAN. Would he accept such a letter?

CALAIH. I will make my mark on it.

STEPHAN. I have no sums of money or riches. I cannot even give you a betrothal ring.

CALAIH. Fine then. I do not like objects dangling on my fingers and arms.

STEPHAN. You do not?

CALAIH. No.

STEPHAN. Then would you take that star for your ring?

CALAIH. Which one?

STEPHAN. That small, very bright one.

CALAIH. The one up there?

STEPHAN. Yes.

CALAIH. If you give it to me, I will take it forever.

STEPHAN. I give it to you.

CALAIH. I will go tell my cow. *(She exits. He follows her.)*

Scene 6

A cold morning in the middle of winter at the Letter Writer's.
The Letter Writer sits behind his desk talking to Calaih.

LETTER WRITER. You say you want to send a message to the High Lord?

CALAIH. Yes, that is what I want to do. But I have not learned how to do writing ... so I come to you.

LETTER WRITER. Yes. I see. What kind of paper do you prefer?

CALAIH. Paper? It makes no difference.

LETTER WRITER. No difference. Certainly you do not want to send a message to the High Lord on coarse brown parchment. It would be an insult. You would appear a fool.

CALAIH. Something nice then. Something he would like.

LETTER WRITER. Let me see. I believe this elegant French scroll paper would be proper. It has a rich smooth texture with a colorful handpainted border. Here, you may touch it if you like.

CALAIH. Yes, it is very pretty.

LETTER WRITER. Now I believe gold ink is what you want. Any other would appear common on such fine paper as this. *(Handing her a sheet of lettering.)* Here, look at these lettering samples. See which you prefer.

CALAIH. *(Looking at lettering.)* I do not read — I cannot tell. Mmmm — this looks nice.

LETTER WRITER. Let me see. What! Block style? For a letter in gold ink to the High Lord? This is the lettering used when someone has lost a horse or a pig; this is the lettering used to denote the color of a cow's hide or the spots on swine. Block style is not something to be used on handpainted imported French scroll to be delivered to the High Lord.

CALAIH. Very well then. You pick it out. I tell you I do not read. I do not know these different kinds of lettering and what is best. All I know is I have an important message that I must send right

104

away to the High Lord, I do not know how to write so I come to you to write it for me. It is midwinter, my cow is waiting for me out on the streets; he will be cold.

LETTER WRITER. I am aware it is midwinter. I did not know you had a cow waiting for you on the streets. Tell me your message. I shall write it down quickly and recopy it later in a way I think suitable. I can have it delivered too if you want.

CALAIH. Yes, do.

LETTER WRITER. There will be an extra fee.

CALAIH. Yes.

LETTER WRITER. So, tell me — what is this message?

CALAIH. Yes, the message. Let me see. Ah ... Dear High Lord, I humbly thank you for your proposal to be wedded with me on the last night of late winter. Yet I tell you I am unable to accept this ... engagement, as I am betrothed to Stephan the Shoemaker's Son. We are to be wedded in the early spring when he returns from Nalesca, where he is building a cottage for us both. *(She stops, waiting for the Letter Writer to catch up. She then continues spontaneously.)* In the village of Nalesca he will be no longer Stephan the Shoemaker's Son — but Stephan the Shoemaker, and I will be his wife, Calaih the Cow Herder. *(Pause.)* As you have expressed such fondness for my hair, I would be happy to cut it off and send it to you in a box. Please let me know your wishes. Your Humble Servant, Calaih, Orphan of Joshua the Cow Herder. There.

LETTER WRITER. Do you really want this sent?

CALAIH. Yes, it must be sent. You must send it.

LETTER WRITER. Very well then, make your mark. *(She does so)* It will cost you a great deal. What with the fine paper and ink and lettering that you have chosen. It will cost perhaps more than a cow herder's orphan can pay.

CALAIH. *(Removing comb from her bag.)* Here is a silver comb for the payment. Look, there is even a design on it.

LETTER WRITER. Mmmm. Where did you get this?

CALAIH. It was a gift to me. *(Pause, as he examines it suspiciously.)* Look here, you may have this brush too if you want. *(He looks at the brush.)* I would not want to keep it for myself — though Taretta might have liked it.

LETTER WRITER. Mmmm. Very well. I will write up your letter as we have planned in exchange for this silver brush and comb.

CALAIH. And deliver it too?

LETTER WRITER. Yes, it will be delivered.

CALAIH. Thank you. Good day.

LETTER WRITER. *(As she is leaving.)* Yes, and good day to you too.

Scene 7

Early evening on the last night of late winter in Taretta's room above the tavern. Taretta is wearing her seductive robe. Her hair is unkempt. She is sick and pale. Her arm is wrapped in red velvet. Alexton calls from outside.

ALEXTON. *(Off.)* Taretta — *(She starts, then begins dabbing perfume generously onto her arm.)*

TARETTA. Yes, come in.

ALEXTON. *(As he enters.)* Taretta —

TARETTA. Ah, Alexton. You are early. It is not yet dark. You may get undressed if you like. It has been some time since I have chosen you. Forgive me, but I have been in great demand these past weeks. *(Standing up weakly, supporting herself on the chair.)* I will make it up to you though — you know I shall. Come, do my breasts still make you tremble? *(He stares aghast, taking in her total dissipation.)* So, show me the gifts you bring and we will begin.

ALEXTON. I have brought no gifts. You have not been in demand. No one has been coming here to you. They all say you are sick with a rotting disease.

TARETTA. Liars. They are liars.

ALEXTON. Why do you wear that red velvet on your arm?

TARETTA. I told you — it is the style of France.

ALEXTON. I do not believe you. Take it off and let me see. *(Coming toward her, trying to grab hold of her arm.)* Let me see your arm. Take this off! I insist — let me see —

TARETTA. Let go. Let go! Do not touch my arm. *(She breaks*

106

away, trembling in pain.)
ALEXTON.   *(Recovering himself.)* Here is my advice to you, Taretta. Go to the Blacksmith's. He is skilled with an axe; his blades are sharp. He is quick and accurate. I tell you this because, unlike all the rest, I once cared something for you. I do not want to see you dead in the morning.
TARETTA. Get out.
ALEXTON. Yes, but before I go, I would like my wife's autumn headdress. There has been no peace in my family since I gave it to you some time ago. My wife has beaten my dog to death with a stick, and we have been very miserable ... I must have it back. I will pay you a fair price for it ... Are you going to answer me?
TARETTA. Yes. I will get it — but you must do something for me. You must tell them I am well, that they can come to me. Horace the Tavern Keeper, he will not let them up. In the mornings he tells me I am through, that they do not want to come. But that is a lie — he will not let them up. You go tell them. Get Casta the Miller — tell him I will bite and lick his big red ears, tell him that. And to Heilington make a noise like this, slurp, slurp, slurp, slurp, slurp ... He will know what I mean, slurp, slurp.
ALEXTON. No one will come, Taretta — they know you are diseased and they have no use for you. Now give me the headdress and I will leave.
TARETTA. No use for me. No use for Taretta — the Woman of Flaming Nights!
ALEXTON. Taretta, the headdress.
TARETTA. Get out. You get out, you worm, or I will break this bottle across your mouth. You tell them to look for me when it turns dark. *(Alexton leaves.)* I have something for them to hear.

Scene 8

Early evening on the last night of late winter at the sisters'
cottage. Calaih is seated at the table sewing her wedding
dress, eating cheese and singing. She finishes sewing, stands
and puts the dress up to her, checking the fit. She continues to
sing. Mardian Enters with the two Guards behind her.

MARDIAN. Your hair is so lovely this evening. Are you ready to go?
CALAIH. What —
MARDIAN. Get your things together. It is time to go.
CALAIH. To go —
MARDIAN. Why do you stand so stunned? Is it not the last
evening at the end of winter, the night of your marriage to the
High Lord? Come, where are your things? Do you have anything
to take?
CALAIH. No.
MARDIAN. The High Lord has asked me to see that you bring
your silver brush and comb so that he may brush and comb out
your fine hair late tonight.
CALAIH. I do not have them — they are lost — I have lost them.
MARDIAN. Indeed. How careless you were to lose them.
CALAIH. Yes.
MARDIAN. Well, come then. We must prepare you for the
ceremony.
CALAIH. Did the High Lord not get my message?
MARDIAN. What?
CALAIH. I sent him a message. Do you not remember?
MARDIAN. A message?
CALAIH. Yes. After the message was sent, the marriage procla-
mation, they took it down from the Great Wall.
MARDIAN. Did they?
CALAIH. To have this proclamation taken down — does this not
mean something?

MARDIAN. Nothing, perhaps, except the paper was worn and could not stand the strength and ice of the late winter's wind. Come now, there is much to be done before the ceremony. *(She takes hold of Calaih's arm.)*

CALAIH. Please, wait — he must have gotten my message — I took great trouble to send it properly. It was written on beautiful fine paper, the ink was of real gold. It was to be delivered to him.

MARDIAN. Perhaps there was such a message.

CALAIH. Oh! So, he must know that tomorrow morning Stephan is returning from Nalesca, where he has built our home. We are to be married.

MARDIAN. If the High Lord has received any such message, he has chosen to disregard it. Come. I can wait no longer. There is no time for further arguments. *(She motions for Guards. The following speeches of Mardian and Calaih occur simultaneously.)* You must be cleaned and bathed and scrubbed with a brush. The dirt must come out of your nails and the wax from inside of your ears. You must be powdered and perfumed and oiled and your hair must squeak and shine and be brushed and braided as the High Lord has demanded.

CALAIH. *(As the Guards come for her.)* But the proclamation was taken down from the wall. No further announcements were made — I cannot go now — I have my own plans. Look, here is my wedding gown. That small bright star you see in the sky — it is my betrothal band — he gave it to me, it is mine — let go. Stop it — you are tearing my gown! Wait — let go of my hair! Ahh — I despise you. I despise you! Stop! Stop! I will go then. I will go.

MARDIAN. There now. Take her to the carriage.

CALAIH. Please — could I take my cow? I want my cow.

MARDIAN. I am sorry; but there is no room for a cow in your carriage. *(The guards lead out Calaih as Mardian follows.)*

Scene 9

In the night on the last day of late winter at the tavern. Lights go up on Taretta, who is covered with grotesque make-up and dressed in garish undergarments with red velvet wrapped around her.

TARETTA.   So, you have no use for me. Alexton tells me that none of you have any more use for me. Is that so? Very well, but let me tell you too, that I have no need or use of you. Do you think I sit up in that room every night and wait for you to come to me — that I dress, adorn and perfume myself just to sit alone waiting — listening to your grunting noises below? Let me tell you that I do not sit long ... I leave in the dark down the back stairway to the outside, to the meadows and the fields. There are many warm bulls and rams and beasts living in these hills and valleys. I have no need of human flesh. I enjoy the smell of the ram's rough fur. It arouses me. It is not stale with sour ale and age, like the skin I bounced with above this tavern. It is warm and pure. I savor the taste and texture of dirt and hair in my teeth and nostrils; and the clutching of hooves on and at my breasts. The tongue of a bull is wet and thick wrapped all around my neck, as I lay on my belly holding tight to the twisting horns. Often the bulls have made me bleed and bleed until my gown and the ground are filled with dark blood. I turn on my back and stare up at the sky pressing my fingers over rocks, earth, roots. My God how I am satisfied. Finally; forever satisfied. I do not need you. I do not want you. Nothing you have can fill me.

Scene 10

In the night on the last day of late winter in the dressing chamber at the castle of the High Lord. Calaih sits in a straight-back chair. Her long hair is braided. Her hands are tied. Mardian is standing over her, trimming the ribbons on her bridal headdress with silver shears.

MARDIAN. There — that will make it the right length. How beautiful! Now I must tell you that the High Lord has heard of your behavior in the bath. It is distressing to him that you would scratch and bite that poor maiden's face. He wishes to speak with you before the ceremony. He would not like to see his bride binded up with ropes. I do not blame him. *(She begins cutting ropes with shears.)* I warn you, do not move from that chair. There are guards at the door. *(She exits. Calaih sits alone. The High Lord enters. He is average looking and jovial. He is eating dried apricots.)*
HIGH LORD. Mmmmm — lovely, lovely, lovely. What hair. Tonight I will brush it out for you. Would you like that? Here, take a piece of fruit. An apricot. No? *(He eats it himself.)* So, they tell me you are unhappy — there was some unpleasantness in the bath. Let it pass, I say — let it pass. All we want is your happiness. Your happiness. I just wanted to make certain you knew that. How I stand in awe of your glorious tresses. They are glorious. Now tell me, have you any requests to make before the ceremony? Any at all?
CALAIH. Did you get my message?
HIGH LORD. Message?
CALAIH. Yes.
HIGH LORD. Yes. Yes, I received it. Thank you for thinking of me. The paper was exquisite, simply exquisite. The text of the letter was a bit disappointing as I recall, but then I am not marrying you under the pretense of any intellectual prowess. It is your hair I find so bewitching, enchanting. Now, if there is nothing more, I must leave you until the ceremony. Farewell. Wait, I will leave this

fruit here, if you should chance to change your mind. *(He places fruit on dresser and leaves. She looks at fruit, then catches sight of the shears. She grabs the shears and puts them down the front of her undergarment. Mardian enters with a robe.)*

MARDIAN. Here is your bridal robe. It is time to dress for the ceremony. *(As she puts the robe on Calaih.)* Now you have met the High Lord, do you not see the foolishness in all your anguish and hysteria? He is handsome and jovial, is he not?

CALAIH. Yes, he is. We shall be very happy together.

Scene 11

Late night in the late winter at the Blacksmith's door. Taretta is pale and shaking, her hair is wild. She wears a long cape wrapped tightly around her.

TARETTA. Let me in. Please, can I come in? I am sick. I need your help. I am freezing out here. I am dying. I tell you I am dying. Will you come — Blacksmith — will you come? *(Blacksmith comes out.)* Can you help me? I have heard that you are skilled with an axe. That your blades are sharp and your strokes are clean and accurate. I have need of such skills.

BLACKSMITH. And what have you brought for me to chop?

TARETTA. My arm, Blacksmith, my arm. *(She holds up arm, then collapses. He carries her inside.)*

Scene 12

In the late night of the late winter in the grand hall at the High Lord's castle. Upstage, perhaps on a higher level, stands Mardian, the Apothecary, and one of the Guards, who wears a priest's robe. They all hold medallions. they are chanting. The High Lord enters, and the chanting stops. He sits on his throne. There are several moments of silence, then music begins playing. Calaih enters slowly in her bridal robe. The High Lord smiles at her. She stops a few feet in front of him, grabs out the silver shears and cuts off her braid.

CALAIH. There is my fine hair that you want so much. It is dead now — dead like a crimson snake. I am glad. I hate it. *(The High Lord rises from his throne, steps forward and pulls the braid from between her fingers, kissing the braid longingly. Slowly, he looks up at her then comes to her.)*
HIGH LORD. You stupid swine! *(He grabs her by the shoulders, then begins biting off her ear.)*

Scene 12a

On another level in the background ... the Blacksmith prepares for the removal of the arm ... He brings in Taretta who is now delirious, sharpens blade, uncovers arm, and raises the blade on the High Lord's line, "You stupid swine!" he swings as the High Lord attacks Calaih. Taretta begins screaming, and the lights dim to blackout as Calaih and the High Lord struggle and Taretta screams. In the blackout, the screaming stops, and we hear the High Lord's voice.

HIGH LORD'S VOICE. Here is your ear on the floor, if you want it.

Scene 13

Early morning, the first day of spring at the sisters' cottage. Calaih comes in. She is wearing the white undergarment and has a white cloth tied like a scarf around her head. The scarf is dark with blood on the side of her head where her ear has been removed. She carries a bloody handkerchief with her ear wrapped inside. She drops the handkerchief on the table and sits down. She is shaking with numbness. After a moment, she sees her wedding dress on the floor and goes to put it on. She is muttering to herself.

CALAIH. My cow. My cow. Why do they murder you? My cow, my dear cow. *(She has just gotten the torn dress on, though not hooked or buttoned, when Taretta enters. Taretta's face is white. With her one arm she holds her cape around her.)* They let me go, Taretta. I am not to be burned. They let me go.

TARETTA. Yes, I see.

CALAIH. Did you see though — what they did to my cow — out there in the yard?

TARETTA. I saw.

CALAIH. Help me get hooked, please. Stephan will be here soon. He will not mind about the ear. He cares so much for me. In time the hair will grow and cover it up. No, he will not mind about the ear. Please, hurry. Can you not use both hands?

TARETTA. Calaih, Stephan the Shoemaker's Son will not be coming here this morning.

CALAIH. Why? Did you see him? *(Taretta nods.)* What did he tell you?

TARETTA. Nothing. He told me nothing. I only saw his head; it was dangling from on top of a pole outside the Great Wall.

CALAIH. Dead ... dead ... Stephan — dead. *(She begins kissing her gown, then she begins tearing at it, ripping it off. Finally she throws it across the room and sits on the floor, holding and rocking herself.)* I have nothing. Everything has been taken from me. Nothing.

TARETTA. Try not to despair, Little Calf. I too have had many things taken from me this evening.

CALAIH. What?

TARETTA. My arm. My arm was cut off.

CALAIH. Really? Was it cut off?

TARETTA. Without my arm there is no one who will want me. I have no work. No way to make money. I suppose I will have to live here forever.

CALAIH. So will I.

TARETTA. We will grow old together. In the winter we will eat hot porridge. You will feed berries to the birds, and I will learn to sew with one hand and my teeth. I will always wear capes; short capes or long capes but always a cape to cover this nub.

CALAIH. I will keep my hair cropped off this way. I do not want it back.

TARETTA. It will be peaceful here.

CALAIH. I am sick with weariness.

TARETTA. If only we had the strength to sleep.

115

CALAIH. Yes, if I could only close my eyes for a moment. *(She rocks back and forth.)* Just for a moment … close my eyes. *(They stare ahead as the lights fade. A tinny old blues song such as "Basin Street Blues" is heard playing in the distance.*)*

The End

* See Special Note on Songs and Recordings on copyright page.

PROPERTY LIST

Medallions
Stick (CALAIH)
Cream, mirror (TARETTA)
Gold fan, silk, earrings, purple rock, headdress (ALEXTON,
    TARETTA)
Money pouch (ALEXTON)
Cheese (CALAIH)
Silver hairbrush (CALAIH)
Bags of money (TARETTA)
Milk, glass (CALAIH)
Scroll (MARDIAN)
Potion, bandages, tub (APOTHECARY)
Satchel (STEPHAN)
Papers, pens, lettering sheet (LETTER WRITER)
Silver comb (CALAIH)
Perfume (TARETTA)
Sewing things, wedding dress (CALAIH)
Silver shears (MARDIAN, CALAIH)
Dried apricots (HIGH LORD)
Long red braid (CALAIH)
Ax (BLACKSMITH)
Bloody handkerchief with ear inside (CALAIH)

NEW PLAYS

★ **THE EXONERATED by Jessica Blank and Erik Jensen.** Six interwoven stories paint a picture of an American criminal justice system gone horribly wrong and six brave souls who persevered to survive it. "The #1 play of the year...intense and deeply affecting..." –*NY Times*. "Riveting. Simple, honest storytelling that demands reflection." –*A.P.* "Artful and moving...pays tribute to the resilience of human hearts and minds." –*Variety*. "Stark...riveting...cunningly orchestrated." –*The New Yorker*. "Hard-hitting, powerful, and socially relevant." –*Hollywood Reporter*. [7M, 3W] ISBN: 0-8222-1946-8

★ **STRING FEVER by Jacquelyn Reingold.** Lily juggles the big issues: turning forty, artificial insemination and the elusive scientific Theory of Everything in this Off-Broadway comedy hit. "Applies the elusive rules of string theory to the conundrums of one woman's love life. Think *Sex and the City* meets *Copenhagen*." –*NY Times*. "A funny offbeat and touching look at relationships...an appealing romantic comedy populated by oddball characters." –*NY Daily News*. "Where kooky, zany, and madcap meet...whimsically winsome." –*NY Magazine*. "STRING FEVER will have audience members happily stringing along." –*TheaterMania.com*. "Reingold's language is surprising, inventive, and unique." –*nytheatre.com*. "...[a] whimsical comic voice." –*Time Out*. [3M, 3W (doubling)] ISBN: 0-8222-1952-2

★ **DEBBIE DOES DALLAS adapted by Erica Schmidt, composed by Andrew Sherman, conceived by Susan L. Schwartz.** A modern morality tale told as a comic musical of tragic proportions as the classic film is brought to the stage. "A scream! A saucy, tongue-in-cheek romp." –*The New Yorker*. "Hilarious! DEBBIE manages to have it all: beauty, brains and a great sense of humor!" –*Time Out*. "Shamelessly silly, shrewdly self-aware and proud of being naughty. Great fun!" –*NY Times*. "Racy and raucous, a lighthearted, fast-paced thoroughly engaging and hilarious send-up." –*NY Daily News*. [3M, 5W] ISBN: 0-8222-1955-7

★ **THE MYSTERY PLAYS by Roberto Aguirre-Sacasa.** Two interrelated one acts, loosely based on the tradition of the medieval mystery plays. "... stylish, spine-tingling...Mr. Aguirre-Sacasa uses standard tricks of horror stories, borrowing liberally from masters like Kafka, Lovecraft, Hitchcock...But his mastery of the genre is his own...irresistible." –*NY Times*. "Undaunted by the special-effects limitations of theatre, playwright and *Marvel* comic-book writer Roberto Aguirre-Sacasa maps out some creepy twilight zones in THE MYSTERY PLAYS, an engaging, related pair of one acts...The theatre may rarely deliver shocks equivalent to, say, *Dawn of the Dead*, but Aguirre-Sacasa's work is fine compensation." –*Time Out*. [4M, 2W] ISBN: 0-8222-2038-5

★ **THE JOURNALS OF MIHAIL SEBASTIAN by David Auburn.** This epic one-man play spans eight tumultuous years and opens a uniquely personal window on the Romanian Holocaust and the Second World War. "Powerful." –*NY Times*. "[THE JOURNALS OF MIHAIL SEBASTIAN] allows us to glimpse the idiosyncratic effects of that awful history on one intelligent, pragmatic, recognizably real man..." –*NY Newsday*. [3M, 5W] ISBN: 0-8222-2006-7

★ **LIVING OUT by Lisa Loomer.** The story of the complicated relationship between a Salvadoran nanny and the Anglo lawyer she works for. "A stellar new play. Searingly funny." –*The New Yorker*. "Both generous and merciless, equally enjoyable and disturbing." –*NY Newsday*. "A bitingly funny new comedy. The plight of working mothers is explored from two pointedly contrasting perspectives in this sympathetic, sensitive new play." –*Variety*. [2M, 6W] ISBN: 0-8222-1994-8

DRAMATISTS PLAY SERVICE, INC.
440 Park Avenue South, New York, NY 10016 212-683-8960 Fax 212-213-1539
postmaster@dramatists.com www.dramatists.com

NEW PLAYS

★ **MATCH by Stephen Belber.** Mike and Lisa Davis interview a dancer and choreographer about his life, but it is soon evident that their agenda will either ruin or inspire them—and definitely change their lives forever. "Prolific laughs and ear-to-ear smiles." –*NY Magazine.* "Uproariously funny, deeply moving, enthralling theater. Stephen Belber's MATCH has great beauty and tenderness, and abounds in wit." –*NY Daily News.* "Three and a half out of four stars." –*USA Today.* "A theatrical steeplechase that leads straight from outrageous bitchery to unadorned, heartfelt emotion." –*Wall Street Journal.* [2M, 1W] ISBN: 0-8222-2020-2

★ **HANK WILLIAMS: LOST HIGHWAY by Randal Myler and Mark Harelik.** The story of the beloved and volatile country-music legend Hank Williams, featuring twenty-five of his most unforgettable songs. "[LOST HIGHWAY has] the exhilarating feeling of Williams on stage in a particular place on a particular night…serves up classic country with the edges raw and the energy hot…By the end of the play, you've traveled on a profound emotional journey: LOST HIGHWAY transports its audience and communicates the inspiring message of the beauty and richness of Williams' songs…forceful, clear-eyed, moving, impressive." –*Rolling Stone.* "…honors a very particular musical talent with care and energy… smart, sweet, poignant." –*NY Times.* [7M, 3W] ISBN: 0-8222-1985-9

★ **THE STORY by Tracey Scott Wilson.** An ambitious black newspaper reporter goes against her editor to investigate a murder and finds the *best* story…but at what cost? "A singular new voice…deeply emotional, deeply intellectual, and deeply musical…" –*The New Yorker.* "…a conscientious and absorbing new drama…" –*NY Times.* "…a riveting, tough-minded drama about race, reporting and the truth…" –*A.P.* "… a stylish, attention-holding script that ends on a chilling note that will leave viewers with much to talk about." –*Curtain Up.* [2M, 7W (doubling, flexible casting)] ISBN: 0-8222-1998-0

★ **OUR LADY OF 121st STREET by Stephen Adly Guirgis.** The body of Sister Rose, beloved Harlem nun, has been stolen, reuniting a group of life-challenged childhood friends who square off as they wait for her return. "A scorching and dark new comedy… Mr. Guirgis has one of the finest imaginations for dialogue to come along in years." –*NY Times.* "Stephen Guirgis may be the best playwright in America under forty." –*NY Magazine.* [8M, 4W] ISBN: 0-8222-1965-4

★ **HOLLYWOOD ARMS by Carrie Hamilton and Carol Burnett.** The coming-of-age story of a dreamer who manages to escape her bleak life and follow her romantic ambitions to stardom. Based on Carol Burnett's bestselling autobiography, *One More Time.* "…pure theatre and pure entertainment…" –*Talkin' Broadway.* "…a warm, fuzzy evening of theatre." –*BrodwayBeat.com.* "…chuckles and smiles of recognition or surprise flow naturally…a remarkable slice of life." –*TheatreScene.net.* [5M, 5W, 1 girl] ISBN: 0-8222-1959-X

★ **INVENTING VAN GOGH by Steven Dietz.** A haunting and hallucinatory drama about the making of art, the obsession to create and the fine line that separates truth from myth. "Like a van Gogh painting, Dietz's story is a gorgeous example of excess—one that remakes reality with broad, well-chosen brush strokes. At evening's end, we're left with the author's resounding opinions on art and artifice, and provoked by his constant query into which is greater: van Gogh's art or his violent myth." –*Phoenix New Times.* "Dietz's writing is never simple. It is always brilliant. Shaded, compressed, direct, lucid—he frames his subject with a remarkable understanding of painting as a physical experience." –*Tucson Citizen.* [4M, 1W] ISBN: 0-8222-1954-9

DRAMATISTS PLAY SERVICE, INC.
440 Park Avenue South, New York, NY 10016 212-683-8960 Fax 212-213-1539
postmaster@dramatists.com www.dramatists.com

NEW PLAYS

★ **INTIMATE APPAREL by Lynn Nottage.** The moving and lyrical story of a turn-of-the-century black seamstress whose gifted hands and sewing machine are the tools she uses to fashion her dreams from the whole cloth of her life's experiences. "…Nottage's play has a delicacy and eloquence that seem absolutely right for the time she is depicting…" –*NY Daily News.* "…thoughtful, affecting…The play offers poignant commentary on an era when the cut and color of one's dress—and of course, skin—determined whom one could and could not marry, sleep with, even talk to in public." –*Variety.* [2M, 4W] ISBN: 0-8222-2009-1

★ **BROOKLYN BOY by Donald Margulies.** A witty and insightful look at what happens to a writer when his novel hits the bestseller list. "The characters are beautifully drawn, the dialogue sparkles…" –*nytheatre.com.* "Few playwrights have the mastery to smartly investigate so much through a laugh-out-loud comedy that combines the vintage subject matter of successful writer-returning-to-ethnic-roots with the familiar mid-life crisis." –*Show Business Weekly.* [4M, 3W] ISBN: 0-8222-2074-1

★ **CROWNS by Regina Taylor.** Hats become a springboard for an exploration of black history and identity in this celebratory musical play. "Taylor pulls off a Hat Trick: She scores thrice, turning CROWNS into an artful amalgamation of oral history, fashion show, and musical theater…" –*TheatreMania.com.* "…wholly theatrical…Ms. Taylor has created a show that seems to arise out of spontaneous combustion, as if a bevy of department-store customers simultaneously decided to stage a revival meeting in the changing room." –*NY Times.* [1M, 6W (2 musicians)] ISBN: 0-8222-1963-8

★ **EXITS AND ENTRANCES by Athol Fugard.** The story of a relationship between a young playwright on the threshold of his career and an aging actor who has reached the end of his. "[Fugard] can say more with a single line than most playwrights convey in an entire script…Paraphrasing the title, it's safe to say this drama, making its memorable entrance into our consciousness, is unlikely to exit as long as a theater exists for exceptional work." –*Variety.* "A thought-provoking, elegant and engrossing new play…" –*Hollywood Reporter.* [2M] ISBN: 0-8222-2041-5

★ **BUG by Tracy Letts.** A thriller featuring a pair of star-crossed lovers in an Oklahoma City motel facing a bug invasion, paranoia, conspiracy theories and twisted psychological motives. "…obscenely exciting…top-flight craftsmanship. Buckle up and brace yourself…" –*NY Times.* "…[a] thoroughly outrageous and thoroughly entertaining play…the possibility of enemies, real and imagined, to squash has never been more theatrical." –*A.P.* [3M, 2W] ISBN: 0-8222-2016-4

★ **THOM PAIN (BASED ON NOTHING) by Will Eno.** An ordinary man muses on childhood, yearning, disappointment and loss, as he draws the audience into his last-ditch plea for empathy and enlightenment. "It's one of those treasured nights in the theater—treasured nights anywhere, for that matter—that can leave you both breathless with exhilaration and…in a puddle of tears." –*NY Times.* "Eno's words…are familiar, but proffered in a way that is constantly contradictory to our expectations. Beckett is certainly among his literary ancestors." –*nytheatre.com.* [1M] ISBN: 0-8222-2076-8

★ **THE LONG CHRISTMAS RIDE HOME by Paula Vogel.** Past, present and future collide on a snowy Christmas Eve for a troubled family of five. "…[a] lovely and hauntingly original family drama…a work that breathes so much life into the theater." –*Time Out.* "…[a] delicate visual feast…" –*NY Times.* "…brutal and lovely…the overall effect is magical." –*NY Newsday.* [3M, 3W] ISBN: 0-8222-2003-2

DRAMATISTS PLAY SERVICE, INC.
440 Park Avenue South, New York, NY 10016   212-683-8960   Fax 212-213-1539
postmaster@dramatists.com   www.dramatists.com